DIESTERWEGS
NEUSPRACHLICHE
BIBLIOTHEK

WILLY RUSSELL

Educating Rita

Teacher's Book

by
Albert-Reiner Glaap
with
Suggestions for Classroom Work
by
Gunther Volk

VERLAG MORITZ DIESTERWEG
Frankfurt am Main

ISBN 3-425-09099-2

Satz: Publishing Service H. Schulz, Dreieich
Druck und Bindung: graphoprint, Koblenz
Printed in Germany

CONTENTS

Preface

Educating Rita. Teacher's Book is divided into four main divisions. The first section supplies additional background information and supplementary material. The second section offers two different approaches to the play, illustrates the author's perspective with reference to two interviews and discusses various versions of the play – stageplay, film and video. The third section is an attempt to pave the way towards integrating the play into different units. Suggestions for Classroom Work and Tests (fourth section) and a Select Bibliography conclude this book.

As the new annotated edition of *Educating Rita* is a revised and updated version of the edition published in 1984, the comments and study aids in this book have accordingly been revised, modified and enlarged. Background information about the Open University as well as the data of Willy Russell's biography have been updated. Some non-fictional texts have been added which may help towards a more thorough discussion of both the context that *Educating Rita* stems from and the language in which the play is written. An important addition is also a recent interview which the editor conducted with Willy Russell in 1996. Moreover, suggestions for an interpretation and a discussion of the play (also in comparison with Bernard Shaw's *Pygmalion*) are integrated into these study aids, such as scene-by-scene summaries, headlines and subscenes.

Needless to say, this book is not to be understood as an obligatory guideline. The play itself shows the direction and recommends diverse, individual approaches. Therefore, the suggestions have merely ancillary functions, they may provide additional help.

I should like to express my gratitude to those who gave assistance of one kind or another. First to Janice Probert-Gromüller, Karin Feilen, Ingrid Hartmann-Scheer and Gunther Volk who have provided ideas and texts for this book. Very special thanks go to Gunther Volk and Nicholas Quaintmere, because they have also written material for *Approaching the Play in Class* and for *Suggestions for Classroom Work and Tests.* Walter Böhmer and Nicholas Quaintmere have proved to be meticulous proof-readers. The editor particularly wishes to thank them both for their co-operation. My greatest debt is to Meike Kuhlmann, my enthusiastic and energetic editorial assistant, who has not only put the text into the computer, but also co-ordinated and commented on various versions of the manuscript with great attention to detail. Finally, it would be remiss not to thank Barbara Drauschke (Moritz Diesterweg Verlag) for being my constant companion during the production process.

I am delighted to dedicate this new edition of *Educating Rita* and the accompanying *Teacher's Book* to a man who has been a very dear friend for more than twenty years, to Willy Russell, in the year of his fiftieth birthday.

A.R.G.

1. Information

1.1 Summary of the Play

Educating Rita[*] is a two-hander about Rita, a 26-year-old hairdresser, throwing off the shackles which tradition has fastened to the wife by laying down the role she has to play in marriage. She is treated by her husband in a condescending manner because she hasn't given birth to a child. She registers for a Humanities course at the Open University. Frank, her tutor, is a university lecturer with a disillusioned outlook on life. He regards himself as a miserable teacher and a would-be poet. The bottles of whisky he hides on his bookshelves take up so much space that the books are apt to tumble down any minute. The play reflects the dichotomy often experienced by students who find themselves more or less in a Scylla and Charibdis situation. On the one hand they have to cope with the rigid routine of training and on the other they would like to choose a more spontaneous approach. *Educating Rita* is about education and personal choice. Rita says of her husband: "He thinks we've got choice because we can go into a pub that sells eight different kinds of lager. He thinks we've got choice already: choice between Everton an' Liverpool ..." (p. 40).

Rita makes use of a different kind of choice. She is an uneducated, yet alert product of the working class in northern England. She very soon recognizes that she doesn't have to keep on being what she has been until now. She is not unlike Beatie in Wesker's *Roots*. But in Rita's case political enthusiasm has been replaced by a yearning to learn. As she wants to get on, she dives headlong into an Open University course, completely against the will of her husband who is solely interested in her coming off the pill and finally taking up her role and having a child. She approaches English literature in a naive and reckless manner. Not having the slightest basic knowledge, she regards such titles as *Howards End* by E.M. Forster and *Of Human Bondage* by Somerset Maugham as filthy and perverted. She associates the poet's name Yeats with Yates Wine Lodge in Liverpool. She sees everything which she is confronted with in literary texts in the light of her own experience. Her lack of reflection in analyzing literature results in some rather strange reactions on her part.

---

* For the title: Cf Section G in the interview (16 October 1996), pp. 52

She is thrilled at being able to define the term assonance: "It means gettin' the rhyme wrong" (p. 14).

When she is given the assignment to write an essay on the question: "How would you resolve the staging difficulties inherent in a production of Ibsen's Peer Gynt?" she writes down a single sentence on the page: "Do it on the radio" (p. 33). But her hunger for life and thirst for learning can move mountains. She hasn't bought herself a new dress for a year, instead she took the course. She only intends buying herself some new clothes after she has passed her first examination. But then it should be a costume, the kind educated women wear who know the difference between Jane Austen and Tracy Austin.

Rita's tutor, Frank, is enthusiastic about the interest she shows, regards however her manner of approach to literature as superficial and highly subjective. She doesn't finish reading Forster's *Howards End* because, as she says, Forster didn't care about the miserable living conditions of the poor thus ignoring the daily problems in life. In his rebuke to her, Frank points out that when writing essays of a literary nature, reference must be made to secondary literature consulted on the subject: "... criticism is purely objective. It should be approached almost as a science. It must be supported by reference to established literary critique ... In criticism sentiment has no place" (p. 24).

In the forthcoming tutorials Rita becomes a new person: she acquires the relevant terminology, but unlike Frank does not allow herself to become possessed by this language. She learns how to deal with literary texts in a critical manner, but her spontaneity suffers as a result.

Frank, initially a trained expert in literary ciriticism, is a tainted, warped expert in the end. Although his academic smugness increases, only alcohol can ease his mental suffering, which springs from the insight that he has failed as a poet. Their personal situations have been reversed. In the beginning Frank is Rita's only glimmer of hope; in the end she is the only living being in his arid environment.

Russell's play is about education, and "real education is about choice", says Russell. "And choice means more than having eight kinds of lager in the pub ... The play is about giving people the confidence and the skills to make decisions about what to value and what to do with their lives."

This is certainly not utopian. And in the face of growing unemployment and public spending cuts, it is important to keep repeating it.

1.2 Background Material

The Students' Book of *Educating Rita* contains both biographical data (pp. 100-101) and an updated list of Willy Russell's work (p. 102). In *The Willy Russell Story* reprinted on the following pages of this Teacher's Book we get some more information "from the horse's mouth". This playwright is reluctant to make statements on his work. His comments in *Contemporary British Dramatists,* however, provide an insight into why and what he wants to write:

[...] I am loath to make any specific statement on the nature of my work as I reserve the right to dismiss on Thursday the statement I made on Wednesday. However, in a letter of 1984, written to a BBC producer to explain why I would not be writing a play I wrote the following (I think for me it will remain as true on a Thursday as it is on a Wednesday):

To write a play one must passionately believe in something which one wants to communicate. The writer might want to tell of the ills of the world, or of his love for another, of society's folly, of mankind's goodness and baseness. He may want to argue a political cause or just show off his wit. Whatever, it is something which requires a passionate belief in telling what one has to tell. [...]

What do I want to say? What moves me? What story do I want to tell? I believe that every play I have ever written has, ultimately, been one which celebrates the goodness of man; certainly, the plays have included emptiness, despair, possibly even baseness. But it is the goodness that I hope the audience is left with. I really don't want to write plays which are resigned, menopausal, despairing, and whingeing. I don't want to use any medium as a platform for displaying the smallness and hopelessness of man. Man is man because madly, possibly stupidly but certainly wonderfully, he kicks against the inevitability of life. He spends his life looking for answers. There probably are no answers but the fact that man asks the questions is the reason I write plays. [...]

(St. James Press, Detroit, 1994, pp. 622-623)

Playwright Willy Russell, author of modern classics such as *Educating Rita* and *Shirley Valentine,* talks about the brick walls that he faced when in the 1970s he attempted to go back to study as an adult.

"In 1967 I was, of all things, a ladies hairdresser. Like hundreds of thousands of people in this country I'd been 'no good at school' and had drifted into a job, because if you're 'no good at school' you have to pay the price and take whatever you can get. I suppose that's fair enough. Even if I'd been given the chance of going back to being a kid again, I still wouldn't have taken advantage of it."

Learning

"When I was at school I simply didn't want to learn the vast majority of what they wanted to teach. I could read and did read a lot. Reading was a pleasure and was never, for me, consciously associated with school or learning. What time was there for learning? What desire was there for learning when learning had nothing to do with reality?"

While hairdressing, Willy realised that he wanted to be a teacher and therefore went back to College to study for O-Levels.

"Walking into Kirkby College of Education clutching *Animal Farm, Henry the Fifth,* and *Browning's poetry,* riddled with fear and uncertainty, the smells common to all educational buildings – making me feel sick with memories of school. It was all a mistake. I'd never be able to do it."

But he did and he fell so in love with studying that he decided he wanted to go on to higher education to take a full-time course. So then he had to fight the Local Education Authority to get a grant.

"I had to accept it, I was never going to get a grant. After some hasty consultation with my wife, we established that if we took in some lodgers, we'd be able to manage without me earning for a year. I was assured that even if the authority would not give me a grant, they would at least pay my college fees."

Financial Situation

"I sat on one side of a table in a room in a Further Education College in Liverpool, opposite me was the Principal. I had not said a word. He glanced up from my papers, dismissed them and began: 'And would you like to tell me why I should let you come to this college? You wasted your time at school. Quite simply son, if you think you're going to waste my time and the time of my staff, you'd better think again.'

Faced with such open hostility I fell to bits. To have organised the whole financial situation and be faced with this wall left me reeling. I would not say a word in my defence. I wanted to tell him that I was a different person from the kid at school. But I just ran."

"At the Education office I told the man I would no longer be treated as a leper just because I'd been no good at school. I told him that I would not have my dignity stripped from me every time I tried to return to education. I told him I had a right to be helped by him and his department. I told him that I paid rates and national insurance, that I was a human being. I probably threw in The Gettysburg Address and 'Oh to be in England' for good measure."

Adult Education

"When I'd finished, he stared at me and very quietly said: 'Get out!' I punched the wall. He was telling someone to 'phone the police.' On his wall was a college in Childwall advertising the course I'd been seeking. I left before the arrival of the law, jumped a bus, found the College, ran down the drive, found the secretary's office and said: 'Please, I know I've got no appointment, but please can I see the Principal?'

The Vice Principal sat me down, passed me a cup of tea and just said: 'Talk.' 'What about?' 'About yourself, what brought you here.'

Two hours later I walked out with the promise of a place in September. I didn't have a sense of victory, a feeling that I'd won. I walked down the drive with feelings only of gratitude and relief. I suddenly, and for the first time in my life, felt that I had a future."

The situation has, fortunately, changed dramatically since Mr. Russell was seeking an adult education and you will now of course be welcomed into Colleges. We now also have many more support systems for potential and current students such as Welfare and Careers Advisors, as well as the very approachable course tutors. So please don't be afraid of coming to one of our events on Adult Learners' Week, and just think, we might even be able to find you a new future!

(Willy Russell. Originally published by the Sheila Kay Fund, Liverpool.)

The Open University

Material kindly provided by the Open University (Student's Book, pp. 84-92) contains useful information about the university as an institution and about the course Rita registers for. Some of the details will be helpful when planning a thematic unit on Education, in which Russell's play functions as the central text.

Education of Women

What's the use, then, of educating women? First we must determine how their education will be used.

The current discussion of women's education appears to center on several supposedly distinct approaches. We can, for instance, educate the career women, or educate all women with the idea that some (but who knows which ones?) will stake out justifiable claims in man's world of science, business, or the professions. And this is a strategic function of higher education. Without it, colleges would be robbing society of the immense contributions of many highly qualified women. Since comparatively few actually do have professional careers, however, we cannot stop here. The colleges can't be just multimillion dollar siphons.

This leads us to a second possibility: the postponed career. This alternative assumes that many women will go into hibernation long enough to bear and raise children and will then return to their career in their "middle years". Some educators are so concerned with middle-year productivity that they would have women's education concentrate on this point. Lois Irish, for instance, concludes that "what is needed ... is an extension of the student's sights beyond the early romantic stages of her life to the years when her principal occupation ceases to be a full-time job in the home".

The third possibility, the one most frequently ignored or ridiculed, is that of educating women who simply want to be intelligent and perceptive wives, mothers, and citizens.

The college graduate who becomes a housewife is said to suffer from confusion and frustration. According to Carolyn Heilbrun, she is "dropped from the heights of Olympus to the depths of the washing machine." This is nonsense. What man in any profession remains continually, if at all, on the heights of Olympus? College presidents, for example, spend a good part of their time pulling socks out of the stuck guts of academic washing machines. Life just requires these unromantic details.

Miss Heilbrun goes on to say that:

> ... The modern woman, graduating from college at an age entirely suitable to the life pattern of a man seeking his place in the world, finds herself launched, not into the world, but into domesticity. She progresses through diapers to the companionship of other three-year-olds, without privacy, without time to recollect herself, without time *to be*. Ahead lie unplanned years for which she weaves nebulous schemes. She thinks that when her children are old enough she, like Mac Arthur, will "return". Too late she will discover that she is out of touch, out of training, and out of demand, and to be out of demand is to be excluded from that public realm where excellence is honored.

Miss Heilbrun seems to be suffering from that dreadful self-pity that afflicts a good many women who confuse equality with conformity.

(From: Edward D. Eddy, Jr., "What's the Use of Educating Women?"
In: *Saturday Review*, 18 May 1963.)

2. Approaching the Play in Class

There are several possibilities of dealing with *Educating Rita* in an English literature class. The ideal approach would be to see a performance of the play, on stage or on video, and then begin to study the script. For, as Willy Russell says in the "Introduction" to the Students' Book, "I write my plays to be played, not to be studied; if that sounds ungrateful let me add that I don't object to the study of the plays, but they are not primarily written for this; for a playwright the medium is the performance whilst the book is merely a record of the text."

Indeed, reading a play must be different from reading a novel, and this applies to classroom work in particular. Whenever possible, the text of the play should be acted out or read aloud with some of the students slipping into the roles of the play's characters (cf Students' Book, p. 79).

Two different approaches lend themselves to reading and studying Willy Russell's *Educating Rita*. The play can be studied scene by scene thereby following the development of both the two characters and the 'action', but it can also be dealt with as the central text in a thematic unit.

In a **chronological approach** the students could be asked to write summaries of the individual scenes which can serve as springboards for detailed discussions. Examples of such summaries are printed in this chapter. Some of these might also, for a change, be read out to the students so that they can integrate them into a larger context. Another task would be for the students to find an appropriate headline for the scene under discussion and then argue for and against the various suggestions. Some scenes require a detailed analysis because they are more subtle amalgams of two or three stories or topics or actions. In such a case, the subdividing of a scene into so-called subscenes (cf pp.19–23) could help the readers on their way.

A diagram (on p. 65) shows in what way *Educating Rita* may be **integrated into various thematic units**. The play can be part of a unit on "Education in England" with reference to The Open University as an educational institution. It (or part of it) can be compared and contrasted with a thematically related play like Shaw's *Pygmalion* or Wesker's *Roots*. Russell's play may also be discussed in a unit on life and culture in the north of England, Merseyside and Liverpool in particular. "Reading, studying and enjoying literature" is another topic to which *Educating Rita* could make a major contribution.

Regardless of such thematic units, an understanding of *Educating Rita* would be incomplete without considering the play as a love story (cf chapter 2.2 and chapter 4). "I tried very hard to write a love story. I hope I did", are Willy Russell's final words in his Introduction to this edition of the play.

Equally important for an appreciation of Russell's play (and Shaw's *Pygmalion*) are Rita's (Eliza's) accents. A discussion of these accents could even initiate a general debate about accents and to what extent they (still) matter in contemporary English society.

A.R.G.

2.1 Chronological Approach

Scene-by-Scene Summaries

Act I

Scene 1

Frank's office. Here we meet for the first time the play's two characters: Frank, a university lecturer (of the absent-minded professor type), an educated man with a bit of a drink problem who has taken on an Open University student in order to earn some extra money; and Rita, his prospective student, an attractive girl in her mid-twenties from a working-class background who hopes to 'improve' herself through education. In this opening scene Frank is supposed to interview Rita in order to ascertain whether she will be a suitable student but instead Rita does all the talking. The meeting is a clash of cultures where two 'different worlds' collide: Frank's world of intellect and academia and Rita's world of mass entertainment, junk culture, and pulp fiction. Nevertheless Frank is charmed by her and finds her genuine enthusiasm for learning very refreshing.

Scene 2

Rita explains a bit about her background, about her comprehensive school and social pressure to conform to the working class 'norm' (leaving school and getting a job) which had stopped her before from going into higher education. After briefly discussing Rita's essay on

Rubyfruit Jungle the conversation turns to Frank, specifically his personal life, his wife, his girlfriend. At the end of the scene Frank persuades Rita to have another go at reading Forster's *Howards End.*

Scene 3

Rita and Frank are discussing Rita's essay on *Howards End.* Rita is frustrated by her inability to get to grips with Forster. Frank is impressed that she has read three books during the week as well as being at work full-time but tries to explain to her that being well-read means being selective in choice of material – not all books are literature!

Scene 4

Rita and Frank discuss Rita's essay in response to the question "Suggest how you would resolve the staging difficulties inherent in a production of Henrik Ibsen's *Peer Gynt*". Frank tries to explain the principles of academic work. Rita tells Frank a little about the 'culture' in which she lives (housing estates, pubs, the *Daily Mirror*) and Frank uses her experience to help her understand *Howards End.*

Scene 5

Frank wants to know why Rita hasn't brought her essay on Chekhov to class. Rita explains that her husband has burnt it along with all her books because he has found out that she has started taking the contraceptive pill again without telling him (despite the fact that she had promised him they would try for a child). Rita's determination to carry on is only strengthened by this. Nevertheless instead of working in class she asks Frank about his private life. Rita persuades Frank to accompany her to the theatre to see an amateur production of *The Importance of Being Earnest.* Frank goes willingly: he misses no opportunity to flirt with Rita.

Scene 6

Frank finds Rita in his office at lunch-time in an excited state. She has been to see *Macbeth* at the theatre and wants to tell him how she feels about it. Frank tries to use *Macbeth* to explain how a tragedy (Macbeth's inability to escape his destiny) is fundamentally different to a tragic event (a perm going wrong, or a man being killed by a falling tree). Frank invites Rita and her husband to dinner.

Scene 7

Frank wants to know why Rita didn't turn up to his dinner party. Rita tries to explain that Denny (her husband) did not want to come and that she was scared she would feel out of place amongst Frank's cultured friends. However, after turning up at his house and being too scared to go in she has, instead, gone to the pub where she has met her husband and friends but she no longer fits in there either.

Scene 8

Rita arrives at Frank's office with a suitcase, her husband has given her an ultimatum "give up studying, or leave" and she has decided to move out. Frank explains that Rita's *Macbeth* essay was powerfully moving but still academically worthless. Frank is beginning to be reluctant to change Rita's unique approach to literature but Rita is determined that she will learn the academic conventions.

Act II

Scene 1

Rita has been away to summer school and is really excited. She feels she has really learnt a lot and is beginning to understand literature and how it is studied. Frank tells Rita his summer was less satisfactory. He has split up with his girlfriend after an argument about eggs but they have got back together. Rita has moved into a new flat with a girl called Patricia (Trish). Frank decides that they will start their term by looking at one of the great poets (William Blake) and is rather taken aback to find that Rita is already very well acquainted with him.

Scene 2

Rita comes into Frank's office speaking in what she considers to be a cultured accent. Frank is horrified. Rita reverts to her normal voice and then relates how she has met a group of students and acquitted herself admirably in a discussion about D. H. Lawrence. One of them has invited Rita to go to France over Christmas and Frank is worried that Rita has already fallen in love with him. Frank tells Rita that her latest essay is at least on a par with those of his other students.

Scene 3

Frank is drunk and Rita does not think he is fit to conduct a tutorial. Frank insists and they discuss Rita's essay on Blake's poem *Blossom.* Frank feels that Rita has taken his initial advice to use academic method too far and although her work is good it now lacks any of her own personality or views.

Scene 4

Rita is late for her tutorial because she has been discussing Shakespeare with friends. Frank tells her that he has found out that she is no longer working at the hairdresser's; she tells him that she now has a job in a bistro. Frank is upset that he and Rita do not seem to communicate on a personal level any more; he feels that as Rita is becoming more and more self-sufficient (in an academic sense) he is losing her; she does not need him any more. Frank gives Rita two volumes of his own poetry and asks her to write a criticism.

Scene 5

Rita arrives at Frank's office, she thinks Frank's poetry is wonderful and has discussed it with her friends, who agree. Frank is furious; he thinks his poetry is pretentious rubbish. He is angry that Rita has learned the 'rules' of literature without really learning to think about what literature is. They argue and part on bad terms.

Scene 6

Frank is trying to get in contact with Rita (who has now reverted to her real name – Susan). He phones her at work and then leaves a message with her flatmate, Trish.

Scene 7

Rita comes to Frank's office to make up and give him a Christmas card to say thank you for the help he has given her. She finds that Frank is being sent to Australia for two years as punishment for one too many alcohol-related incidents and is in the process of packing up his personal effects. Rita thanks Frank for making her look beyond the mere process of studying literature (learning quotes and so on). Frank gives Rita a dress that he has bought previously (presumably for another lady friend of his) and Rita wants to give Frank something in return. The scene, and play, ends with Rita finally giving Frank the haircut that she wanted to give him in the opening scene.

Nicholas Quaintmere

Headlines

Act I	**Scene 1**	Rita meets Frank or: innocence meets experience.	(7-20)
	Scene 2	First steps in an unfamiliar environment.	(21-29)
	Scene 3	Pulp fiction vs. good literature.	(30-32)
	Scene 4	Learning the rules of the game and trouble at home	(32-37)
	Scene 5	Strains in Rita's marriage; Frank's growing disillusionment.	(38-44)
	Scene 6	Learning the difference between tragic and tragedy.	(44-48)
	Scene 7	Alienated from friends past and present.	(48-51)
	Scene 8	Pains and dangers of becoming educated.	(51-53)
Act II	**Scene 1**	A changed Rita is beginning to see things from a new perspective.	(54-62)
	Scene 2	Rita's metamorphosis and Frank's bout of jealousy.	(62-65)
	Scene 3	Frank and Rita are moving in opposite directions.	(65-69)
	Scene 4	A lesser known English poet tormented by jealousy.	(69-71)
	Scene 5	Student and teacher come to blows over Rita's interpretation of Frank's poetry.	(72-74)
	Scene 6	Two phone calls interrupted by black-outs.	(74-75)
	Scene 7	Looking back and looking ahead.	(75-78)

Gunther Volk

Subscenes

Act I	**Scene 1**	**Rita meets Frank or: innocence meets experience**	(7-20)
	1.1	The phone call	(8)
	1.2	Rita is different from the "proper students".	(9-15)

- the picture (9-10)
- getting into the O.U. (10)
- poetry you understand (11)

	• reasons for enrolling (12)	
	• swearing (12-13)	
	• testing the professor (13)	
	• assonance (14)	
	• name change (15)	
1.3	A hairdresser who is serious about her course.	(16-19)
	• Mrs S. White	
	• Difficult customers who "wanna walk out a different person". (16-17)	
	• Domestic reason for enrolling. (17-19)	
1.4	Frank does not want to teach Rita.	(19-20)
Scene 2	**First steps in an unfamiliar environment**	(21-29)
2.1	A jammed door to a tastefully furnished room.	(21)
2.2	Reasons for enrolling in an O.U. course.	(22-24)
	• Reasons why Rita did not attend university after school.	
	• Peer pressure and working-class values. (23-24)	
	• Postponing the buying of a new dress. (24)	
2.3	Rita's first essay.	(24)
	• **Criticism 1:** "Criticism is purely objective … In criticism sentiment has no place."	
2.4	Frank's personal circumstances and his poetry.	(26-27)
2.5	A professor who obviously fancies his mature student Rita.	(28-29)
Scene 3	**Pulp fiction vs. good literature**	(30-32)
	• Bring in other authors.	
	• **Criticism 2:** Not all books are literature.	(31)
Scene 4	**Learning the rules of the game and trouble at home**	(32-37)
4.1	The ritual of answering exam questions.	
	• **Criticism 3:** An essay is more than just a sentence. It must contain "some considered argument" and "outline your reasons … with quotes from accepted authorities." (34)	
4.2	No meaning of life, no culture.	(35-36)
	• Beer out of plastic glasses.	
	• Vandalism.	

	• Wrong values from the media and the unions.	
4.3	Denny is opposed to Rita becoming educated.	(36-37)
Scene 5	**Strains in Rita's marriage; Frank's growing disillusionment**	(38-44)
5.1	A jealous husband and a wife who feels alienated.	(38-40)
	• Getting "life" from literature. (39)	
	• Rita wants "choice". (40)	
5.2	A disillusioned professor goes to the theatre with Rita.	(42-44)
Scene 6	**Learning the difference between tragic and tragedy**	(44-48)
	• Rita discovers Shakespeare.	
	• Frank invites Rita to dinner at his house.	
Scene 7	**Alienated from friends past and present**	(48-51)
	Row with Frank and Rita's identity crisis.	(50-51)
	• "I don't want to be myself." (50)	
	• "I can't talk to the people I live with anymore." (50)	
	• "There are better songs to sing." (51)	
Scene 8	**Pains and dangers of becoming educated**	(51-53)
8.1	Dilemma 1: "Either I stop comin' here an' come off the pill or I could get out altogether." (51)	
8.2	Dilemma 2: If you want to succeed at the O.U., you'll have to change.	
	• "You're going to have to suppress, perhaps even abandon your uniqueness. I'm going to have to change you." (53)	
	• **Criticism 4:** "It's a totally honest, passionate account of your reaction to a play ... But in terms of what you're asking me to teach you of passing exams ... in those terms it's worthless." (52)	

Act II	**Scene 1**	**A changed Rita is beginning to see things from a new perspective**	(54-62)
	1.1	Back from summer school in London.	(54-56)
	1.2	Changes in Frank's and Rita's lives. • Julia left Frank in France. • Rita moves in with her fashionable flatmate Trish. (57)	(56-57)
	1.3	"This room needs airing." • Rita wants to be taught outside. • Discovers the stuffiness of Frank's room. • Learns to hold her own against Frank. • "Your going is as inevitable as – as …" (59)	(58-60)
	1.4	A dead good poet: William Blake's *The Blossom.* • The student has moved beyond her tutor's control. • The two characters are moving in opposite directions: Rita is becoming increasingly sophisticated, Frank increasingly disillusioned with academia.	(60-62)
	Scene 2	**Rita's metamorphosis and Frank's bout of jealousy**	(62-65)
	2.1	A change of voice.	(62-63)
	2.2	No longer wary of the real students.	(63)
	2.3	Frank's bout of jealousy. • **Criticism 5:** "Oh – it – erm – wouldn't look out of place with these. … Dead honest." (65)	
	Scene 3	**Frank and Rita are moving in opposite directions**	(65-69)
	3.1	A decline in Frank's personal and professional fortune. • Use of swear words, slang expressions. • Rita's 'education' of Frank is becoming more apparent.	(65-66)
	3.2	Rita's essay on *The Blossom.* • A subjective Frank disagrees with Rita's objective interpretation. ("I don't like it.") • **Criticism 6:** "You seem to assume that this poem is about sexuality. … it's up to the	(67)

minute, quite acceptable trendy stuff about Blake; but there's nothing of you in there." (67)
- "Don't keep treatin' me as though I'm the same as when I first walked in here." (68)

Scene 4 **A lesser known English poet tormented by jealousy** (69-71)

From hairdresser's shop to bistro – from boring, insignificant detail to "things that matter". (70)
- Assignment: "A critical assessment of a lesser known English poet. Me." (71)

Scene 5 **Student and teacher come to blows over Rita's interpretation of Frank's poetry** (72-74)

5.1 Frank's creation, Rita, shows off her knowledge of English literary criticism.
- "This is brilliant. They're witty. They are profound. Full of style."
  "You can see in it a direct line through to 19th century traditions of – of like wit an' classical allusion." (72)

5.2 Frank's devastating criticism of Rita. (75-76)
- **Criticism 7:** "you recognize the hallmark of literature now, don't you? ... Why don't you just go away? I don't think I can bear it any longer." (73)

Scene 6 **Two phone calls interrupted by blackouts** (74-75)

Scene 7 **Looking back and looking ahead** (75-78)

7.1 Frank's nadir: a two-year-sabbatical for making a night of it. (75)

7.2 Rita looks back and ahead.
- Realization: "I just ended up with a load of quotes ... I wanted it all so much that I didn't want it to be questioned." (76)
- "Because of what you'd given me I had a choice." (77)

Gunther Volk

2.2 Thematic Approach

Central Topics for Analysis

Some of the topics that could be at the centre of the discussion are:

1. Rita – a representative of the Northern urban working class
2. Rita's education and her study of literature
3. The development of Rita's character
4. Rita's language

With reference to these headings, a few suggestions for classroom work will be made in the following comments. These comments merely serve the purpose of drawing attention to lines, paragraphs and scenes in the text that could be brought into focus when discussing the play.

Re 1: Rita – a representative of the Northern urban working class
Rita is a typical representative of the Northern urban working class. She is a cheeky Liverpool girl hungry for education. Her real name is Mrs Susan White (p. 15). She is married to Denny whose sole interest is to talk her into coming off the pill and having a baby. He expects her to play the role ascribed to her by the arid rules of the "working-class culture". On several occasions Rita refers to the characteristic features of that culture, e.g.:

> Rita: […] I don't see any, y' know, culture. I just see everyone pissed, or on the *Valium,* tryin' to get from one day to the next. Y' daren't say that round our way like, cos' they're proud. They'll tell y' they've got culture as they sit there drinkin' their keg beer out of plastic glasses. […] (p. 35)

Scenes 1 and 4 of Act I illustrate Rita's working-class origin. Watching TV when there is a fad on, reading the *Daily Mirror* and *The Sun*, buying new dresses – these are only a few symptoms of the working-class culture, as Rita sees it. The people of her social class think they have got choice because they can go into a pub that sells eight different kinds of lager or because they can choose between Everton and Liverpool, "between one lousy school an' the next, between lousy jobs or the dole, … between *Stork* an' butter" (p. 40).

Rita works in a ladies hairdresser's where she meets many people of her own class, women who "never tell y' things that matter. Like y' know, doin' a perm, well y' can't use a strong perm lotion on a head that's been bleached with certain sorts of cheap bleach" (p. 16). These women want to alter or at least improve their appearance, "they wanna be changed" (p. 17). But they get on Rita's nerves, because they don't see that if you want to change you have to do it from the inside. There is no deviating from the conventional rules that have been brainwashed into them like into almost all the people of Rita's surroundings. Later in the play, Rita quotes her husband: "He says there's a time for education. An' it's not when y' twenty-six an' married" (p. 52).

Re 2: Rita's education and her study of literature
Rita considers the life of working-class people to be a disease. She tries to explain to her husband that she wants a better way of living her life. But she knows that "if you want to change y' have to do it from the inside". There are quite a few indications of her willingness to change her life completely. Act I, Scene 2 is most revealing in this respect and should be studied very carefully. Rita is not going to buy herself a new dress until she passes her first exam (p. 24). (At the end of the play [p. 77] Frank presents her with a dress that he bought "for an educated woman friend".) Rita wants to discover herself first and therefore tries to do away with everything that has so far put its stamp on her life. First of all, she changes her name from Susan White to Rita (p. 15). "My mind's full of junk, isn't it?", she says. "It needs a good clearin' out" (p. 32). When she was a child she always wanted to go to a boarding school "with a tuck-shop an' a matron an' prep. An' a pair of kids called Jones minor an' Jones major" (p. 22). But she also points out what, in her eyes, is wrong with education (p. 28). She must still learn that answering examination questions is a ritual, a game with rules (p. 34).

Rita enrols in a literature class. Quite a few misunderstandings arise between her and Frank due to their different levels of knowledge and education:

- Forster – the novelist and critic / Foster – a kind of beer
- Yeats – the poet / Yates – a wine lodge in Liverpool
- Eliot – the poet / Elliot (Ness) – the Chicago copper who caught Al Capone

At first almost every book is a piece of literature to her. Maugham's *Of Human Bondage*, D.H. Lawrence's *Sons and Lovers*, and *A Stone For Danny Fisher* by Harold Robbins are mentioned in the same breath (p. 31). Rita is completely unfamiliar with the demands and methods of literary criticism. Her approach to literature is an appreciation or partisan interpretation, as Frank puts it. He claims that criticism is never subjective and "must be supported by reference to established literary critique"

(p. 24). *Howards End* is "crap" to her, because the author, in his ivory tower, did not deal with the conditions of the poor in his novel. He couldn't care less (p. 25). Literature, in Rita's eyes, should be an image of real life. She interprets a literary text in the light of her own experiences of life. There are three scenes which illustrate Rita's difficulties in analyzing literature and in handling the knowledge she has acquired.

In Act I, Scene 2 Frank tries to get his concept of literary criticism across to his protégée.

Reading Literature

(Rita) ←	→ (Frank)
– appreciation	– criticism
– sentimental	– purely objective
– subjective	– supported by reference to established critique
– partisan interpretation	

Life and Literature

(Rita) ←	→ (Frank)
– Forster couldn't care less	– you cannot interpret E.M. Forster from a Marxist viewpoint
– is not concerned with the poor	– literature can ignore the poor
– in his ivory tower	
– *Howards End* is crap	

In Act I, Scene 6 Rita tells Frank about a performance of Shakespeare's *Macbeth* that she saw on the previous evening. This can be the starting-point for a discussion of the characteristics and implications of "tragedy" as a literary term.

(Rita)		(Frank)
I've left a customer with a perm lotion. If I don't get a move on there'll be another tragedy.	→	Which might be quite tragic – but it won't be a tragedy ... the tragedy of the drama has nothing to do with the sort of tragic event you're talking about, ... the sort of thing you read in the paper that's reported as being tragic, "Man Killed By Falling Tree", is not a tragedy.

It is for the poor sod under the tree. → Yes, it's tragic, absolutely tragic. But it is not a tragedy in the way that *Macbeth* is a tragedy.

In Act I, Scene 8 Frank attempts to make Rita see that an emotional statement about a certain experience cannot be considered a stepping-stone to success in an examination.

Re 3: The development of Rita's character
Rita breaks away from a world where people do not want to change. She discovers a new way of looking at the world. There are a few scenes in the play that indicate stages in her development. As early as in Scene 5 of Act I she points out that she has cut her family ties. With reference to her husband she says to Frank: "He even brings me presents sometimes, hopin' that the presents'll make her come back. But she can't, because she's gone, an' I've taken her place" (p. 39). In Act I, Scene 7 she tells Frank why she did not come to the dinner which Julia had organized in Frank's house. When she had found the house and walked up the drive, she says, she saw Frank's guests through the window sipping drinks, talking and laughing. At that moment she realized that she couldn't go, that she did not belong to them, that she was a half-caste. Moreover she did not just want to be someone who is funny, charming and delightful. She did not want to play the court jester.

Rita's development is also reflected in her growing influence on Frank. In Act II, Scene 1 Rita presents her tutor with an expensive pen on which the following words are engraved: "Must only be used for poetry. By strictest order – Rita". She tries to talk him into writing poetry again, and from now on takes the initiative: "What are we doin' this term? Let's do a dead good poet" (p. 57).

The fact that she can recite a Blake poem from memory marks a further stage in her development. In some performances this is underlined by Rita sitting at Frank's desk and in his chair when discussing Blake's poetry with him. Hand in hand with Rita's development Frank's dependence on Rita's visits and his own adoption of her earlier naive criticisms increases. To a certain extent their roles are even reversed. Now it is Rita who makes statements like "It becomes a more rewarding poem when you see that it works on a number of levels" (p. 67) or "You're being subjective" (p. 67). This development culminates in Scenes 4 and 5 of Act II, when Rita insists, with all the emphasis at her command: "I understand literary criticism" (p. 71) and "I'm educated, I've got what you have an' y' don't like it because you'd rather see me as the peasant I once was" (p. 73).

Re 4: Rita's language

Rita is not merely characterized by her actions but also by her way of speaking. Special emphasis should therefore be laid on an examination of the characteristics of her language which are partly adopted by Frank later in the play. The following examples could serve as a starting-point for the discussion.

- I'm comin' in, aren't I? (p. 9)
- that stupid bleedin' handle on the door (p. 9)
- The poem is dead good (p. 11)
- Pack it in? (p. 12)
- Y' don't mind me swearin', do y'? (p. 12)
- I was off me cake. (p. 23)
- Studyin' was just for the whimps (p. 23)
- This Forster ... doesn't half get on my tits (p. 30)
- What the frig am I trying to do? (p. 50)
- I didn't get narked or anythin' (p. 51)

For other examples see *Educating Rita*: Footnotes (pp. 7–78).

A.R.G.

A Love Story?

Willy Russell says in his introduction to the play that he "tried very hard to write a love story". Who loves whom in the play? Does the student have a crush on her teacher or is the teacher in love with his student? The following quotations shed light on the love angle of the play.

page:		
13	Rita:	If I'd got some other tutor I wouldn't have stayed.
20	Frank:	I don't want to do it. Why come to me?
	Rita:	Because you're a crazy mad piss artist who wants to throw his students through the window, an' I like you. ... Don't you recognize a compliment?
26	Rita:	Are you married? What's your wife like? Why did y' split up?
28	Rita:	If you were mine and y' stopped out for days y' wouldn't get back in.

Frank: Ah, but Rita, if I was yours, would I stop out for days?

29 Frank: What I'd actually like to do is take you by your hand and run out of this room forever.
Frank: Why didn't you walk in here twenty years ago?

30 Rita: This Forster ... doesn't half get on my tits.
Frank: Good. You must show me the evidence.

38 Rita: You'd think I was having a bloody affair the way he behaves.
Frank: And aren't you? ... Perhaps your husband thinks you're having an affair with me.

39 Frank: Do you love him (Denny)?

42 Frank: I am going to the theatre with ravishing Rita.
Rita: I'm not gonna try an' rape y' in the middle of *The Seagull.*
Frank: What an awful pity. You could have made theatre exciting for me again.

47 Frank: What are you doing on Saturday? ... I want you to come over to the house.

52 Stage directions: Frank takes hold of her and tries to guide her to the chair DR.
Rita (breaking away from him)

59 Frank: What do I do when, in appalling sobriety, I watch you walk away and disappear?

60 Frank: I shall be glad to see you go.

64 Frank: You can't go (to the South of France). ... Is there much point in working towards an examination if you're going to fall in love and set off for the South of ...

67 Frank: You seem to assume that *The Blossom* is about sexuality.

67 Rita: It becomes a more rewarding poem when you see that it works on a number of levels. ... You're being subjective.

67 Frank: ... There's nothing of you in there.

68 Frank: Because *I* care for you – I want you to care for yourself.

69 Rita: I work in a bistro now.
Frank: You didn't tell me.

It struck me that there was a time when you told me everything.

70 Frank: Is Mr Tyson one of your customers?

73 Frank: Why don't you just go away? I don't think I can bear it any longer.

76-77 Frank: It (Australia) is a paradise for the likes of me. ... Why don't you come as well?

The quotations make it obvious that Frank is infatuated with his student. Rita may have led her tutor to believe that she "likes" him (20). Later in the play, however, she tells him in unambiguous terms that she has not got any time "for an affair. I'm busy enough findin' meself, let alone findin' someone else. I don't want anyone else." (38)

The love angle of the play is important in that it helps explain why Frank becomes dissatisfied with the academic progress his student has made in Act II. Instead of congratulating her on how well she has internalized what he set out to teach her in Act I, he now dismisses her objectivity in literary criticism. His disillusionment with Rita becomes apparent when he disagrees with her over the sexual interpretation of *The Blossom.* It reaches its climax when he criticizes Rita for applying the rules of objective literary criticism to his own poetry. What he secretly wished for was the sort of spontaneous emotional, highly subjective response that Rita used to show when she first walked into his office.

Looking at Rita's academic progress in terms of what the Open University course expected her to accomplish, she is undoubtedly a success. In terms of Frank's emotional expectations of her, however, she has failed. This is why he calls himself Mary Shelley, thus implying that he has created a monster.

Gunther Volk

Does Accent Matter?
The Pygmalion Factor

John Honey

[...]

What reconciles me to the gradual and eventual passing of accent varieties in Britain is my awareness that accent differences are one of the greatest obstacles to genuine social equality in this country. So long as accents persist, they will be made the excuse for some people to discriminate against others and belittle them. It is no accident that the USA, where a much larger proportion of the population speak with a standard accent (General American) than is the case with RP (Received Pronunciation) in Britain, is plausibly regarded as a much more open and genuinely democratic society than our own. A similar judgement has been made on Australia, where nearly everybody speaks with the same accent, though in a varying degree of breadth.

There is a simplistic argument which says that rather than requiring the child to adapt to society, we should change society to accommodate the characteristics to the child. Those who use this argument to deny children access to any awareness of the implications of speaking with one accent rather than another are doing them an obvious disservice, if they cannot also guarantee that society's attitudes will have changed in time for that generation of children to benefit. Sadly, such a guarantee is impossible, if only because, as I have repeatedly stressed, accent involves a more complex set of judgements than mere snobbery.

A few years ago I was invited to take part in a programme on a local radio station, in which, along with another professor, I discussed the significance of accents with two groups of teenagers, one from a south-east London comprehensive and the other from a public school. One fourteen-year-old black girl expressed, in very vehement terms, her disbelief that her very strong Cockney accent could ever entail any kind of prejudice or disadvantage in her life: she had already discovered that she could go down into the neighbouring London borough and find plenty of young people who spoke as she did and accepted her as one of themselves. My professional colleague urged her equally strongly to disregard anyone who might suggest that the ability to speak only in this one accent could carry any disadvantage. Though I was not given an opportunity to say so, I could think of many situations in which this strong local accent would limit her chances in life, certainly if she stepped outside the boundaries of her local community and its immediate vicinity. It was ironic that the advice was given her by a professor who had himself made the transition from a local London accent to the RP without which he would have been very unlikely to have secured his professorship. Moreover, he had chosen a neighbourhood in which to live, and schools for his children to attend, which ensured that they too did not have to go through life speaking as he was encouraging this young teenager to persist in doing.

What is really at issue is a child's right to an 'open future'. By discouraging that girl from expanding her repertoire of accents to include a standard one, we are determining in advance the kind of opportunities of work, social contacts, and lifestyle generally she will be able to enjoy.

The presuppositions of Shaw's *Pygmalion* in 1912 were echoed in a News Chronicle article in 1956 by two journalists, E. Arnot Robertson and Jill Craigie: "If you were a good fairy, hovering over the cradle of an English child today, the most prized gift you could bestow on it would be an impeccable accent." They were echoed again in 1983 by the Cockney comedian Jim Davidson, himself the master of several accents, when interviewed on the Wogan programme on BBC 1 TV. He explained that he wanted to secure a "posh" education for his young son, partly because of the quality of the teaching the boy would receive, and partly because of the "correct" accent he would acquire. [...]

(London: Faber & Faber 1989, pp.174-175)

What Was That You Said?

Tom McArthur

Proper English ain't spoke like it used to be. Now hear 'the New London Voice'.

Tom McArthur, linguist and lexicographer, is editor of the 'Oxford Companion to the English Language' and the scholarly journal 'English Today'. At his home in Cambridge, he spoke with NEWSWEEK's Daniel Pedersen and Deborah Curran. Excerpts:

NEWSWEEK: How healthy is the Queen's English these days? Has the idea that England sets a world standard for spoken English faded away with the empire?

McArthur: Phoneticians refer to the Queen's English as Received Pronunciation, or RP. That isn't so much the accent of the royal family as the middle and upper classes, especially in southern England. It has been put forward as a standard accent, first for England, second for the rest of the world. But it was always a minority usage, spoken by 3 to 4 percent of the population in social positions of great authority and prestige. [Over time,] RP has slowly lost its central position and is being increasingly challenged.

Is there any point to a globally recognized standard for spoken English?

There isn't such a standard, and I doubt there ever will be. English is a bit like an octopus. Its tentacles go everywhere, and new kinds of people take it on. There is no central authority, like the Académie Française. Because it's so dominant and yet so varied, [English] can be both attractive and dangerous – dangerous because it exerts enormous power. There's an enormous suggestion of modernity about English, especially American

English. [And] a print standard tends to hold everything together. People can make their accents approximate to the expectations of others because they read the same printed material.

What about spoken English in England?

A strain is gaining strength that I call the New London Voice. There's nothing really new about it, but it's now common – even fashionable – on radio and TV. It's a compromise voice about halfway between RP and Cockney. No one has done a detailed description of it yet. All we can do is tell anecdotes about it.

What does it sound like?

One thing that distinguishes it is the glottal stop. It's like a catch in your throat that replaces the "t" sound or the "k" sound. It's the way Michael Caine says "little" – not "little" or "li'l" but "li()l". Also, "l" at the end of a word is pronounced "w". The word "technical" becomes "te()nicaw." And "St. Paul's Cathedral" becomes "Spaw's Cathedraw." Younger speakers of RP use these pronunciations, as well as upwardly mobile working-class people from London.

Some say the Princess of Wales and John Major speak this way now. Do you agree?

We're dealing with a continuum. People strung out along it like beads on a string between RP and Cockney. In Diana's case, you will sometimes hear a glottal stop. People of her background 30, 40 or 50 years ago would rather have died than say one. She'll say "li()l" not always, but sometimes. John Major speaks London RP appropriate to his age. People mention him in this context because he talks about a classless society.

Can British speech ever be classless?

Maybe not. But people are more comfortable socially these days, and cross-class communication has become more desirable.

Is an old-style RP accent now a disadvantage in politics and business?

Outside the United Kingdom, a public-school accent may still be very effective. It's still the preferred voice among diplomats. But in the U.K., people don't want to be identified as having elite educations. They want to be part of the gang. The New London Voice is a kind of social lubricant. But I doubt that it will spread much beyond southern England.

But the BBC goes around the world.

Yes, some BBC people use it. But we're tending to get voices with the pace and clarity necessary for radio and television, rather than an accent that is supposed to represent the best possible English for all people in all places.

So no one in India or Singapore should cultivate the New London Voice?

People in India, Nigeria or Singapore have tended to develop their own "educated" accents. They are less and less concerned with how the British speak. All of us, born to the language or who have learned it as the world's lingua franca, will need to adjust to each other when we meet.

Has American English surpassed English English?

The United States is for many people around the world a symbol of modernity. People at the cinema or watching TV are absorbing American English all the time. There are 250 million people in the United States and 57 million people in the United Kingdom. The language's centre of gravity is now nearer Ohio than Oxford. So it's probable that a kind of American accent will become a model for vast numbers of people around the world.

Will the queen use it?

The queen won't change. Prince Charles won't change. But it's impossible to imagine now how a later monarch might speak.

(From: *Newsweek*, 26 April 1993)

2.3 The Author's Perspective

Two Interviews

WILLY RUSSELL IN LIVERPOOL ON 9 MARCH 1982

An excerpt from this interview is contained in the Students' Book, pp. 103-104. (ARG: Albert-Reiner Glaap; WR: Willy Russell)

ARG: Well, let's start with the title of my article. I called it "Educating Rita: Literature for Everyone" meaning (a) that this play should be seen by everyone interested in modern drama and in literature in general and (b) that this play advocates that literature should be written for everybody. Do you agree?

WR: That literature should be written for everybody? Well, literature is written for everybody. What upsets me in England – I mean I've often been provocative at readings and at drama-workshops and one thing and another, and said, "I don't believe in literature," and it is a provocative generalization but there's a lot of truth in it. There's something I call the "literature industry" which has sprung up and which I particularly loathe because it seems to me to put a huge barrier between the Ritas of this world who want to learn and literature itself. It probably comes out in my own sort of situation; for years and years and years I wouldn't pick a classical or known and regarded author from the bookshelves. I'd rather read a racy, accessible American novel or indeed quality American novels because they were rarely classified as literature; you know, you go to the library and they wouldn't be in the literature section. And so I'd read Steinbeck in place of Charles Dickens, which is ludicrous because Dickens is as much in touch whith a working-class culture which I wanted to read about at that time as Steinbeck in America. But I believe, of course, literature should be for everyone because it's packed with ... a lot of it is packed with ... delight and goodness and knowledge and all those things. But a hell of a lot of it is for study; I don't think *that* concept of literature has any place for example on the stage and in the theatre because I think it's anathema to drama. Have I answered that?

ARG: Yes, you have. Thank you. I have the impression that this play was first and foremost an attack on the way literature is dealt with at university level in the sense that it more or less shatters the students' spontaneity if they approach literature the way Frank does, curbing Rita's spontaneity from the start. Am I right in that?

WR: It's not an attack because I'm not damning it, right? I mean Rita attacks Frank for damning it and says: "You take it all for granted. You've got it, you know. You *can* take it for granted. I haven't got it; I'm hungry for it. I want it. I know there's something good in there." But towards the end of the play she does become a parrot-like, literature-spouting literary tart, if you like.

At the end of the play what I'm trying to show is somebody who synthesizes the best of what she can gain from literature and what she can get from *Rubyfruit Jungle* and the books that she just catholicly indulges in, right? One's talking about a complete woman. It's also, of course, something to do with class. I'm talking about somebody synthesizing the best of two classes and trying to attack the divisions really in teaching, in education, and in the class system. And so it's the division and it's the elitist way in which literature is dealt with that I really object to.

ARG: Has the end always been the way we find it in the Samuel French edition. (WR.: no, no, no, no) Could you elaborate on that?

WR: I worked very hard in rehearsals. I knew I hadn't written the end of the play and during rehearsals I actually wrote what I've just said to you about synthesis. Rita, I gave her a four-page speech and the actors went, "Jesus, that's shattering." But it was on the page. It was very good in a *literary* sense, but in a dramatic sense it was out the window. And I kept saying: "But yea, you know, I want to say this. I want to say this in my play." Everybody was supporting me in wanting to do this. But that terrific thing happened that can often happen with actors; they just said, "You know, we can't *play* this; it's good but we can't *play* it." I said: "You're dead right." I went away that night and quickly wrote the final scene as it stands now, took it in the next morning expecting everyone to loathe it and they loved it, because it played well. And what it taught me was, because the second we finished that scene Mark Kingston said: "Look, that's terrific." I said: "Why?" He said because at the end of this play what an audience wants to know is did the two characters get together. "Actually forget your high blown intentions – you're writing a *drama*." And that's always something I'm saying to myself but in the process of writing, you know, one does get carried away thematically and *forgets* that an audience is sitting out there. The Ritas and the Franks actually want to know what happens to the two characters. It's simple, you know. Drama actually always is. Like the best melodies.

ARG: So the thing about the haircut came in later.

WR: Yes, it did. The haircut especially. You see in Liverpool we're in a sort of very fortunate position because I suppose there are many artists and writers who live here, who are in touch with each other; it being a small town we drink in the same places, I mean four of us run a theatre here, you know. So we are constantly in touch with each other. And I remember bumping into Bill Morrison in a bistro, during rehearsals, and I said to him: "How am I going to end this bleeding play?" And he said very jokingly and offhand: "She should cut his hair." I dismissed it as a joke, left it and it was only much later when I was writing this scene I said, "Hold on! If it looks like a come-on – is she going to kiss him or is there some sexual interaction or whatever and we just play a simple joke at the end – that's the way to end the play".

ARG: And the thing about the new dress came in later as well.

WR: I'd always been trying to get that in. I'd been messing with that the whole way through.

ARG: There's some mention of it, because she wants to get a costume that ladies wear who know the difference between Tracy Austin and Jane Austen.

WR: That's right, yea. And so I knew it was a strand of the play that had to be resolved or could be capitalized …

ARG: Some sort of leitmotif in the play, if you like.

WR: Yes, yes.

ARG: I'd like to take up one question that some of my students asked. It's not my question in this case. They took, if I may say so, a dim view of the cynicism at the very end of the play (WR.: cynicism at the end of the play?) on the part of Frank, at least that's how they saw it. I don't know if they got it right. "You found a different song," he said, "and on your lips it's shrill and hollow and tuneless," and they thought this was a fairly cynical approach to ...

WR: I don't. I don't think it's cynical at all. I love him when he says that. He's so positive when he says that because what he's attacking is this woman who has become totally one-dimensional and pseudo-literary. I mean he refers back to the mother's song, doesn't he when he says this?

ARG: That's right.

WR: It's oversimplified; it's a song of real culture; it's a woman, you know, who doesn't think that she's got a culture, who *can* sing; underneath all the layers of working-class valium and deadness there's still something – some little flame alive which occasionally, you know, is fanned and bursts into flame again. Now Rita, when she *walks in* is *wonderful*; I mean she's magic; she's a full, potent human being and as Frank says to her very early on: "I don't know why I want to take you through this; it's dangerous territory, you know." And the worst happens. He is forced because, I suppose, he falls in love with her – I mean on a general level – and so he's forced to go along with it. And his forecast comes true; his prediction comes true; the inevitability sort of comes true, you know; it comes down to roots and you've got a Frankenstein-like figure. And that's how I see her when she comes in and talks about his poetry and she says, you know, it's like writing in the way of the 18th-century tradition of wit – and that's rubbish. So I'm sorry, I disagree with your students and actually I find it worrying they should see it that way.

ARG: They thought, here you've got some sort of stereotyped group of characters. You've got Frank on the one hand who starts out as being an educated person, a man of literature, a man of letters, and he finally ends up being an alcoholic. And you've got Rita on the other hand, who's a fairly spontaneous being, going into literature and she ends up being not really what she should be.

WR: At the very end of the play? Why, at the very end of the play she says, "I've got choice." I mean why should she not be that. Seems to me that's the most complete form of human being you can have.

ARG: So the decisive word is choice at the very end.

WR: Oh absolutely, absolutely. And with Frank; Frank is far more cynical at the beginning of the play than he is by the end of the play surely.

ARG: Would you consider the end of the first Act to be some sort of turning-point of the whole play? I mean the moment when Rita, after having decided not to go to the dinner party, decides to go back to the place where the others are, you know, to her husband and her mother.

She calls herself a freak and a half-caste. Would you consider that to be some sort of turning-point where the roles are reversed?

WR: Not that the roles are reversed, but I don't know what you mean by turning-point. It's what I'd call a cranking-up moment. It's the moment where the drama cranks up on to its next level. The drama's going to be pursued ruthlessly.

ARG: But she leaves everything behind that has been very important to her.

WR: No, she doesn't. Her husband throws her out. It's the point at which she says: "I know I've got to go on," – right? "and damn the consequences." – So that's why I call it a cranking-up moment. It's a pivotal moment in the drama but it's the point at which she says, you know, she decides, doesn't she, she decides that she can't go on and she reports back and she says to Frank, "Now I've decided and I went back to that pub," and if her mother hadn't said to her "We can sing better songs than those," you know the junk she's been singing at the juke-box, then Rita would probably have abandoned the course.

ARG: In the penultimate scene of the first Act, Rita talks to her mother and her mother starts weeping and Denny, her husband, is successful in talking her out of doing this. Rita can't stand this and that's why my students thought she leaves everything behind her.

WR: No, she doesn't. She comes back to take the course. The next scene after that opens with Rita entering with a suitcase and saying, "He threw me out. It was an ultimatum. He said either I stop coming here to you or I could get out all together." The way I direct it, she's in tears. You know, she's a woman who has to go along a certain path and understands that there are other people who are going to be hurt, but she is not prepared to, as she says at some point, she's not prepared to lie down and stop rocking the coffin. She's got to go through with it because she knows the rightness of what she wants to do. She says "I want to ... He says I've betrayed him: I know I have but I could not betray myself."

ARG: Right, and then she takes the initiative. My students weren't too sure about the end of the first Act. They thought that very scene was important because on the one hand she was thrown out, but on the other hand she decided at that moment that where she came from was not really where she should stay; that she should do something different, like taking that literature course; go back to the course and forget all about what had happened.

WR: She regrets that the consequences of her taking this course will ultimately be the hiving-off and the sealing-off from her background. But she regrets it. She's a realist and she's not a sentimentalist. So she knows it's going to happen but, throughout that act, she tried to bring her husband along with her. It's very interesting, you should talk to some other university students in this country. There's nothing more designed to cause a divorce than a woman taking an Open University course if her husband is not educated. I only found this out after the play. It's more of a threat to a working-class male, especially, if a woman becomes educated than it is if she has a sexual affair. Of course I'm indulging in a bit of poetic licence when I say that. There are no exact figures but it's a well-known fact. An Open University student will tell you the same.

ARG: That's very interesting. Very important, too. Do you think there is anything else that they should be given as background information in order to understand this scene and other scenes in the play? Information about the Liverpudlian background and the Open University aspect of the play?

WR: No, they should be able to get it from the play.

ARG: There are a few general questions that were discussed in connection with *Educating Rita*. And after discussing the play as such, the question arose whether education is just a ticket qualifying the particular person for entrance into higher social strata, or is it more than that?

WR: Of course it's far more than that. It is that which demeans education because education becomes merely the acquiring of knowledge to use as a social tool, which is a pole and that is the way, by and large, it is used in this country. And education is so bound up with class, is such a divider in this country, and I don't think Rita wants to use it as a weapon against anybody. I think what she wants is to get the fruit of education without being lumbered with the baggage, but she becomes lumbered with the baggage in the second Act. I've not answered that very well. Ask me again.

ARG: Seeing the play one gets the impression that Rita takes the Open University course in order to qualify for something else, to get what might be a ticket enabling her to enter higher social strata. Is that right?

WR: No, I don't think she wants to enter, for the sake of it, a higher social stratum. I think that what her instinct tells her is that if she enters this *other* stratum, not necessarily *higher*, but this other stratum, she can feed the element inside her which is not being fed in her present social stratum. She says how hungry she is for education. She does want to be able to sit down and discuss books and art and music and to be spiritually fed and, to stay in the metaphor, she feels that she's starving in her present social stratum, that it's arid and that if she moves in this other social stratum it will be some sort of oasis. This was certainly something I felt before I went back to education. I overvalued to a ludicrous extent the idea of education, what, you know, college and higher education was and went through a period being very like Rita, you know, being very boring and suffering from "art in the head". I used to stop people on buses and ask them what they thought of Chekhov which was very boring for them. Poor souls on the buses.

ARG: The question I asked myself when reading the play was: can education be dealt with on its own? Shouldn't it be linked up with politics, somehow?

WR: I think the play is political and I think it's linked to politics.

ARG: Could you enlarge on that? What is the political aspect of it? I mean developments and changes in the field of education are somehow predetermined, as it were, by political decisions, aren't they?

WR: Yes, they are. When I became a teacher (this is probably a sort of side issue but it might answer the question) when I became a teacher I went into teaching because I thought I could actually radically alter certain situations and could effect some sort of change. I thought that teaching was a potent political tool. I found out when I got into education that education was the tail of the dog which was being wagged by the political animal and that one was mostly ineffectual as a teacher because you were the branches, you weren't the roots of the trees, and whatever was decided at root level you had to implement. You know, there was a certain leeway within that. One could, if you like, counter-influence once one was in the classroom, but in the broadest sense of the word one was fairly impotent as a teacher given the prevailing political party of the day. What I mean when I say that the play is political is not political in an obviously ... I mean it doesn't discuss the politics of education; it's the politics of the people involved in the play and it's political because it's discussing class in this country.

ARG: This afternoon we were talking about Shaw's *Pygmalion.* Could we just go over your ideas on that subject again?

WR: It's always amused me when reviews have used *Pygmalion* as a reference to *Educating Rita* and seeing *Rita* as some attempt to rewrite *Pygmalion* because before writing *Educating Rita* I'd never read or seen *Pygmalion*. I suppose I must have been told the story of *Pygmalion*, you know, I must have known of this guy who takes up a girl who can't talk and teaches her how to talk. But there was never any conscious intention to parody because I didn't know it and I remember telling a friend of mine, a poet called Adrian Henri, about the play I was working on. He said, "Ah, *Pygmalion.*" I said, "What!" I thought, "Christ, maybe you know, I'm writing a play which has already been written," which is often the case with a play. So I didn't go to *Pygmalion*. I left it, I finished the play and after I'd finished the play I read *My Fair Lady.* I happened to see a copy knocking about which I suppose is a fair distillation of *Pygmalion*; it's still got the same elements of the story, you know, and I could see why people referred to *Pygmalion*, but I don't honestly think there's much connection there, much conscious connection.

ARG: Yet there is a connection between Rita in *Educating Rita* and Beatie Bryant, as you say.

WR: Yes, there is, there is. Robert Cushman wrote an interesting review which consisted of a comparison between the two plays. Now something like *Roots* was a play that I did see many years ago before I was a writer. I only first started going to the theatre when I was nineteen. I'd never seen a play in the theatre before I was nineteen. But I remember that *Roots* was one of the few plays in the early days which made me think there was something worthwhile in the theatre. But I sort of ... I take, you know, a different line from Wesker. When he wrote *Roots* there was that huge debate in magazines like *Encore*, which I've since read, about working-class theatre and working-class characters in theatre and bla-bla-bla and Beatie Bryant acquiring a voice and Wesker with Centre 42 and that sort of going out to educate the masses and giving them culture. I disagree with that totally. I don't believe that you can give the working class a middle-class culture, because a working-class culture is still based upon the word spoken and not the word written. It's still an oral-based culture and not a literary culture. A middle-class culture is a literary culture; information is carried in the written word. Still today in the working classes the information and the code is dealt with in the spoken word and that's why it's terribly difficult to teach working-class kids, because teaching is a middle-class process: it's conducted by the middle classes with reference to literature ninety-nine percent of the time.

ARG: It might be a good idea if you give some kind of introduction yourself to the students. Is there anything that you would tell the students in a brief introduction to the play, anything you would like to tell them? Not really interpreting the play, just talking about yourself, about your plans etc. Like Ayckbourn on the *middle classes*, you could say *Russell on the working classes* just to give them your idea of what you think the working class is like, or what kind of role it plays in *Educating Rita*.

WR: Yea, it might be that I'll send you a little bit of writing on that rather than do it out of thin air really because it's difficult to generalize. When I do a programme note or a little preface I spend *days* on the thing, you know. I suppose it's to do with ... again I suppose I'm like

Rita. I mean, I think it's very interesting coming from the working class, and writing for the stage, as I do. I write for drama. I write for the spoken word. I don't write for the written word. And you know, the drama has become the preserves of the middle classes and yet really it is a working-class form. I only found out that very late in life.
ARG: There was a time when young people merely went to see movies rather than plays. To a certain extent I think it's still like that. At least in London, if you think of the theatres in Shaftesbury Avenue, there are hardly any young people to be found there.
WR: I can think of two West End plays that have brought young people in over the last eight years. One's *Educating Rita*. You see a lot of young people in there, and the other's *John, Paul, George, Ringo and Bert* which brought young people. You can always tell when it's a young audience because the dear seats are sold last and usually in the West End the twelve-pound seats go quickly because it's the geriatric section. I shouldn't be unkind. I don't mean to be unkind: I'm just using shorthand. And the kids always buy the cheap seats up at the top.
ARG: As my students do not know too much about your earlier work and about the plays that are in the offing, could you elaborate on that?
WR: Well, I write for television a lot as well as writing for stage and treat each medium with equal respect. I don't write bread and butter for television. I tend to write, in fact I've only written, single-shot plays. That's the prestige slot in England where you can write a play. You're not on to some sort of series treadmill and I've never written as part of any sort of group writing exercise for telly. I've just written a five-part thing for television which we are filming at the moment but that is a complete story. It has to be serialized because even with me they wouldn't run it for five hours one night. There's no way. It's a single story is what I mean. I like oscillating between both mediums. The nature of the play tends to dictate the medium. An idea comes to me and I want to write it. I don't sit down and say I'm going to write a telly play. It's when I've an idea, it'll tell me what form it should take. Since writing ..., well, no I'll go back before that: I wrote my first plays when I was a student. They were fairly didactic, short – somebody called them neo-expressionist pieces – but in each of the first three plays that I wrote there was an element of realism and of working-class characters, of writing in the particular idiom I write in, because I use my local language a lot. I've always believed (like Bashevis Singer) that if you write about anywhere, well you are writing about everywhere, and *I tried to write the sort of plays I'd like to go and see.* It's difficult. When I wrote *Educating Rita* I tried to write something very different from what I'd written before. I'd been

commissioned by the RSC to write *a* play. I refused to take, I generally refuse to take, commissions for certain subjects. I say if you want to commission me to write a play *I* write a play. I'll make the decision as to what it's about. You can tell me if you've only got four pounds on the budget or sixty million; that'll affect things. But I tend to just write the play that I want to write. What generally happens, and what happened before I came to write *Educating Rita*, was I sat down and tried to write all sorts of different plays that had become too easy for me to write, and so there was no attraction in me writing them. So I didn't and I spent a long time till I finally got to writing *Educating Rita*. Since writing *Rita*, I've written a television film and the film of *Educating Rita.* I have done a short play called *Blood Brothers* which plays exclusively in schools for fourteen to sixteen-year-olds. I'm just saying this for the benefit of the tape. And now I'm in the process of turning that play into a musical play which will open round about September time at the Liverpool Play House.

ARG: What did you have to change when *Educating Rita* was going to be presented or performed in the United States. Did you have to change anything?

WR: Well, I'd rather not talk about it because I was terribly, terribly compromised by producers, by the RSC [The Royal Shakespeare Company], by agents. I just worked very hard to get myself out of that situation as soon as possible. A production in the States is still pending and what I've done is ask them to have the play translated into American rather than have me do the job. It was Shaw who said, "The one thing that divides the English and the Americans is their common language." We assume it's the same: my God I've never been to a more foreign country than America, and to that end have agreed to have the play translated by a writer called Ntozake Shange who's translating the play into a play about a black American girl, and it seems to me that is the only way to do the play in America because it loses its political potency if you play it as an English play on Broadway that they're paying 30 dollars a seat for. It seemed to me, and I want Ntozake Shange to test my theory really, it seemed to me that the only way in which you would find a parallel for the English working class in America was in the Blacks. You know, in America there's that thing that people are not defined by their language. But the Blacks are. The Blacks have a potent street language like Liverpool has a very potent, identifiable, musical, witty language which comes out of oppression. I think all potent languages seem to come out of some sort of form of oppression. And so it seems to me that that's the only parallel in America.

ARG: This afternoon I mentioned that the play's going to be staged in Germany, and we were discussing the problem of the references and allusions to literature. What would be most in line with your ideas, topicalize it or Germanize it? You can't really cut out those references. On the other hand you can't expect a German audience to understand all these references or allusions.
WR: Well, an English audience doesn't understand, you know, all the allusions. The play's written in a way that you can understand the nature of the scene and exactly what's been said without knowing who E.M. Forster is, without knowing who William Blake is, because you get to understand very quickly in the scene what those authors represent. So I wouldn't worry too much in foreign translations about re-jigging the play, to pander, and I don't mean that in an insulting way, but to pander it to local taste. I don't think that the play needs to pander.
ARG: Thank you.
WR: Thank *you*. And Goodnight!

WILLY RUSSELL IN LIVERPOOL ON 16 OCTOBER, 1996

An excerpt from this interview is contained in the Students' Book, pp. 105-112.

A.

ARG: Talking about Rita, what was it all about the Americans trying to make a black woman out of her?
WR: That was me actually, that wasn't really the Americans, that was me being absolutely as pragmatic as I could be in a certain set of circumstances. The American rights of the play were acquired by a producer and the production of the play had been set up before I even got to know about it. The RSC [The Royal Shakespeare Company] had done this. Within the terms of my contract the RSC were perfectly at liberty to make this deal in Australia and America. In the rest of the world this play was just a monumental success. It's interesting that in two places – well in Australia it wasn't so bad – but in America the play never had a full blown production.
Mike and I got out to New York and met with Larry and Lucy and it was painfully obvious that it would have been imbecilic for us to try and get these actors to play in English, in the English language. It wouldn't work, they didn't have the facility to play in specific regional English. I can never ever watch an English actor on stage play an American. I'm never totally convinced. I remain to be convinced about American actors

playing English – on film yes, but over a two hours journey of a play no. And so it seemed to me ludicrous that we should put these actors and the play through this. So Mike and I, Lucy and Larry met up day after day after day for five days overlooking Central Park and I kept saying: "Just let me hear your voice saying this line." So I Americanised the script, knowing it was just for a three-week production, it was a try out. Knowing there would be no glaring lights and no great press attention one could conduct this experiment without being too damaged if it all went sadly wrong. For whatever reason this play was presented for three weeks and it was sort of o.k., but I knew we'd been compromised and ideally it was not the way to do it. But I also knew we were locked into a situation where we couldn't present the play in New York as an English play that it was going to have to be American.

So at this point I said to the producers, with whom I didn't have a great relationship, let's accept that we have a problem. I want the play to be told in a certain sort of voice. This working-class voice is absolutely specific. It's written on that instrument. What people don't understand, a playwright does not only write words, he writes the sounds of words. A composer writes a part for a cello, and then he comes in and it's being played on a trombone – it can be played by the greatest hornplayer alive – but it's not a cello. So I knew I needed a certain cello sound for this play. And so I started to think what the American equivalent of a working-class Liverpool girl would be. There is a thing that Roddy Doyle says in *The Commitments* about the Dubliners being the white blacks of Ireland. I always thought there was a great affinity between working-class English with say Jewish Americans, where the humour is very similar and/or black America, urban America. So I said to my producers: "If we're going to do this play as an American play it really has to be translated and the spirit of it has to be translated into that language." I talked about the possibility of Rita being Jewish and having that Jewish language – I suppose one was thinking of an early young Barbra Streisand – and I also mentioned the idea of it being in a black community at which point the producers threw their hands up in absolute delight because they knew and admired enormously the work of a writer Ntozake Shange. She wrote a very successful play in the 80s called *For colored girls who have considered suicide/when the rainbow is enuf*, a very very big hit, a sort of Jazz piece, terrific. So it was agreed that I would meet with Ntozake and see if we got on. She was rather frightened of this, because she didn't know if it was politically a) o.k. for her to do this because she's quite an experimental writer she was frightened of working in the mainstream, and b) as a very articulate black woman she was probably worried about the race implications of this. So we met, slightly nervously but we got on famously. We spent a wonderful night in her apartment. Charlie Fuller turned up from the film *A Soldier's Story*, and we were checking each other out and they were checking me out. Ntozake got to work on it and wrote this version of the play. I liked a lot of it, but not everything. By that time my relationship with the producers had broken down irreparably and Ntozake's relationship had broken down irreparably, by which time she was a writer in residence somewhere down in Atlanta. She staged it down there. Some time later somebody wanted to stage this version of the play again and I think I said no, I didn't want it to happen. Not because I didn't admire Ntozake's work on the play, but the whole thing had become so sour. We tried to go down a certain path and we went down it for the wrong reasons, we went down it because we'd been compromised and basically what I should have done was wash my hands off the whole thing, right back on day one, when I learned of this side deal, I should have backed off the whole thing. Very important learning experience for me. There you go that's why there is this version knocking about. Now the play is, and has been for the last ten years, played everywhere on that Stock and Amateur circuit.

B.

ARG: I understand that you hardly ever research certain things, that you write them the way you think they should be written. Is that correct?

WR: Oh yes. Research is probably the most convenient excuse for not writing or in some cases writing badly. I always feel that if I don't know it I can't learn it, I can't go out and study it and write about it. I mean what I do is retroactive, retrospective research. So that with Rita I'd take the idea of the old Open University structure as a means of getting a girl with no qualifications to even go to university into a repetitive tutorial situation with a tutor. I stretched a point and hung it on the Open University and then I checked out with people who taught in the Open University: "Would this be credible?" "Yes." Fine – that's my research done on that. Because if I don't know what I'm writing, I really can't go out and learn it, it has to be within me. When you're really writing, when it's really alive, what happens is the characters start to say things I didn't know I knew. You can't get that out of research. The novel I'm writing at the moment, *Raymond,* I do need to know certain things about agencies that deal with mental illness, what we could call juvenile delinquency, and the

Criminal Justice Bill. Now I need to know these things, but I will not go back to those until I've written the scenes, to touch up on these things. If I go and do all my research now, I will in a sense, become corrupted, my absolute vision of where this character should be going will have to take in other considerations. I'd rather get the universal truth first and then, of course, if the reference is wrong, I'll change it.

C.

ARG: Talking about what went into the making of *Educating Rita,* you said to me in an earlier interview that *Pygmalion* did not play a role in your process of writing. Now students in a number of German schools are to read *Educating Rita* alongside *Pygmalion.* What is your stand on this?
WR: Don't apologise, I'm very flattered that they should put *Educating Rita* alongside Bernard Shaw.
ARG: What do the two plays share and where do they differ, from your point of view?
WR: *Educating Rita* was written unconsciously of *Pygmalion,* I did not know the play. I'd not even seen the film. I suppose somewhere at the back of my head I could have overheard the story of *Pygmalion.* But I didn't, I remember towards the end of writing *Educating Rita* I was in a bar with Adrian Henry, a poet, who asked me what I was working on. I gave him a sort of thumbnail breakdown of the plot and towards the end of this he said to me: "Ah, *Pygmalion.*" And I was terrified: "Don't tell me I've written a play which already exists." I knew of course that Shaw had written a play called *Pygmalion,* but I'd never come across it. I thought I'd wasted all these months and Adrian said: "I'm not talking about *Pygmalion* the play, but Pygmalion the myth." And I could see that. When I finished *Educating Rita* I shot round to my father-in-law's house to get a copy of *Pygmalion* and he didn't have one, but he had a copy of *My Fair Lady,* which I sat down and read. I could see immediately that I'd written, in my unconscious way, in an area that Shaw had gone into, but of course there are fundamental differences in the plays, not just in plot and theme. In Shaw's play it is an experiment conducted by a linguist, whereas I wrote about a girl who demanded an education. But there are parallels. In *Pygmalion* there's that linguistic journey. All I can do, and people may find this difficult to believe, is raise my hand and say: "I did not know of *Pygmalion* when I wrote it." And if I had known about *Pygmalion* I'd put my hand up and say, "Sure, I did." But I wrote *Educating Rita,* because it stands totally separate from *Pygmalion.*

I have to say thinking of *My Fair Lady* – I have yet to read *Pygmalion* […] – which is a wonderful piece of work, sublime music, some great setting of Shaw's work to music, without losing anything of the Shaw. My play differs from *My Fair Lady,* I have to say, principally because the springboard is not this experiment, it is much more a mutual contract between the pupil and her selected teacher. Other differences are that the way it deals with class in the latter end of the 20th century is very different from the way that Shaw was dealing with class, class differences then were much more marked, much more obvious than they are today. Interesting though, that when Eliza walked onto the stage she must have blown the theatre to bits. But *Educating Rita* did the same thing, even way back in the 1980s. So as I talk about it seeking the differences, I seem to find more parallels between these two pieces of work. The tone in the two plays is very different.

ARG: What about the endings?

WR: Again, the ending of *Pygmalion* is very different from the ending of *My Fair Lady,* isn't it? The ending is very very different from what I would write, because I suspect in a sense that I was, at the end of this play, seeking a harmony between these two characters and between the various strands in the play. One of the things I didn't want to do, I was anxious never to do, was to write a play in which knowledge, education were damned, questioned by all means and the way we teach; what education can do, its dangers, its pitfalls, education within an English academic institution, I certainly wanted to explore and criticise that. But I was very anxious that knowledge itself should not be damned which is why at the end of the play there is a very crucial speech from Rita, where she talks about choice, because education equipped her with the means to make those choices.

ARG: But it doesn't solve all the problems, does it?

WR: Of course it doesn't. There is no palliative out there that can sort your life out, including education. You are still that person going through that. And she does, she says: "I will confront my life. I will address the choices I have." And she may very well make the wrong choice. Even if we did that thing looking at her ten years on, you may find she's been able to harmonise and synthesise for herself. Maybe she's somebody who – in a sense like me – can move totally freely between the sort of high academic society that she aspires to and the absolute working-class culture of a terraced house and a pub. She can move freely between them. And she sees, as she does in the play, the qualities inherent and the disadvantages in both those worlds.

D.

ARG: The endings in the film *Educating Rita* and the stage version are slightly different, aren't they?

WR: I think the film ending is a better ending than the play, because you cannot do that on stage. You cannot do that thing of suddenly introducing music. I think that ending pulls out the emotional stops in a way I was unable to do on stage. You have to work within the confines you set yourself on stage, I had to work within an office. Still, let's say even in a theatre we'd been able to fly in a huge walkway and play the scene, what it would have done is to cripple the form of the play. Just as, in the second act, I was finding it increasingly difficult to finish this play and to articulate the play in this room that I'd trapped myself and my characters in. On one occasion I gave in and I brought Denny, Rita's husband, into the play and into that room in order to articulate certain things. I knew it was disastrous, I knew it would never play. You can't have a play in which you establish that the play is going to take place in the terms of two characters and the off-stage characters are evoked by the on-stage characters. Just to bring in and realise one of those off-stage characters would be theatrical suicide.

I had to write the scene with Denny in order for me to learn how to write the scene without Denny. That's what writing a play is like. It's not a question of "Oh, this is what I want to write," and you sit down and just do it. The journey of a play is full of discoveries and full of constant battles between an idea of what you want to say and finding the means to achieve that with what is at your disposal, with the terms of engagement that you set right at the top of the play.

ARG: That's very interesting, because normally when we talk about catalysts, the catalyst is mostly one of the characters of the play or an off-stage character. When you were talking about Denny that makes me think of a catalyst in the creative process. If Denny made you write what you were going to write about, then he was the catalyst in your creative process.

WR: That's right. It was a good scene as well. A terrific scene, but I just knew I couldn't do it, I'd established terms that would not allow me to do that on stage. [...]

E.

ARG: Comparing the film with the stage play, I think that the working-class references in the film version are not as obvious as in the stage version.

WR: I am not the author of the film, I'm the writer of the screenplay. There is in fact a collective authorship of a film, but it's usually in today's age credited to the director, in this case Lewis Gilbert. The director heads a collective authorship. So I can't say to you with anything like the sort of authority that I have as a stage author what I think of the film. I'm reluctant to be openly critical. Had I been the author of the film, I think you would have found that the working-class substructure of the film would have been much more accurate than it is. I think that there is a certain sentimentalising and a romanticism in the film. For example, there is a shot of Rita walking into her street, it's almost a parody of a working-class street, terraced houses, a gas works at the end of it, that I think is very much 1950s Britain, I don't think it's 1980s Britain. I think she could have lived in a completely different setting. The wedding scene felt to me like a more older wedding situation than Rita's sister would have been going through. But I'm not being critical when I say that, I'm just trying to make certain observations. Often these things are absolutely straightforward practical.

The film, for financial reasons, was shot not in Liverpool, but in Dublin. Dublin is a very very different city: the colour of the buses, the fronts of the houses, the nature of the streets, the nature of the light, Trinity college. The other thing is that because of that the actors who played the working-class characters were cast out of Irish acting talent. It means that you've got a lot of actors there – very good actors – but who are trying to cope with a Liverpool accent. It's very difficult for a Dubliner to get a Liverpool accent right, because they're similar and widely different, because of that you get a softening of the working-class side of things. When a voice is not accurate, you always get a softening.

F.

ARG: If we could talk about classroom work for a moment. I've been asked some questions by teachers as to the use of the film as part of a classroom project. Should they read the stageplay first and then see the film as a kind of counterfoil? Should they see the film first, because it provides background information and "local colour"? Or should only specific scenes from the film be used which lend themselves to a contrastive analysis with the respective scenes in the stage version?

WR: They're the teachers, let them do their job. Of course they know their methods of teaching, they've got recourse to those different versions. Use it in whatever way they think is the most effective. I'm not going to offer them the correct prescriptions for the teaching of *Educating Rita* or "Bildung". Let me just say, if I was a teacher, I know what I'd do. I probably wouldn't even go near the text. I would probably work with the kids first, try and get them to create something to do with their own education, be it school education or whatever. I'd get them involved in drama. I'd probably end up with the class acting out a play in the classroom over a number of weeks, the kids playing all the different parts and the script coming largely from them. That's where I'd start.
ARG: Do you know what I did last year, once we're on to this? I took the film and had them look at it, didn't say a word about it, nothing except that it was *Educating Rita* and had them watch it. I asked them: What is this about? And it was fantastic the kind of comments they came up with.
WR: I wouldn't even start with that, I wouldn't even mention *Educating Rita*. Because what I want to start with is let us look first at *our* education, let's look at the German education system, let's look at being in this class today with Willy Russell or Professor Glaap. Let's see attitudes to that and what happens out there etc. I suppose it's that thing that I learned as a teacher trying to teach very different kids than we're talking about here. Most of my kids couldn't even read for a start, barely literate. I've found that in the teaching of history or geography, the best place to start was in their immediacy. Validate the kids so that they feel that they have a tale to tell, that they have a language and then from that you can open up into a wider world, you can move back into a deeper historical world, move towards bigger geographical frontiers. Just start here and now. I know for example from German schools that when Brecht was prescribed, lots of German kids felt that it was just absolutely tedious to study. Now, there is an immediate connection with *Educating Rita*, because when Rita was at school the reason she hated school was she must have had that equivalent in our system of studying something that had no meaning for her, that did not allow her into the subject and fire her with the subject.
One is flattered of course by the fact that so many teachers and students seem to want to study *Educating Rita*, but the subtextual danger within that is that we can breed an entire generation of German kids who hate the work of Willy Russell, because it's taught badly, because they're forced into studying this stuff. You've got to make it come alive. A drama is a live piece of work. Ultimately we can study it, we can put it into the la-

boratory, we can dissect it. I think in an early version, I wrote a speech for Frank – I don't know if it's in the play now – in which he talks about pulling a bird down from the sky, pinning and dissecting it. You might understand from that a lot about a bird, but it's never going to fly in the sky again.

G.

ARG: I'd like to get something clear about the title *Educating Rita*. If I remember correctly it goes back to the title of a radio show, is that right?
WR: Yes. It was *Educating Archie*. It was a programme that was on the radio when I was a kid. They'd play the national anthem before closing down and you were supposed to stand up in your front room. There was no twenty-four hour broadcasting then, radio would broadcast until eight in the evening. In those days of radio variety shows still existed in the theatre and were beginning to make their way onto television. In variety you have all sorts of acts, like the magician, the acrobat, the comedian, the unicyclist, the ventriloquist. The ventriloquist's art depends upon you looking at a man or woman who has a doll on the end of his or her arm and makes it appear that it is the doll speaking and moving. And for reasons I have never been able to understand, a ventriloquist got a radio-show. So there's the ventriloquist and his dog called Archie and you hear them on the radio. You can't see the illusion. It could have been two different characters, it wasn't, it was the same one, because we used to see him on variety shows as well. But it was this guy with a dog called Archie, a rather upper-class, little snotty dog and the programme was called *Educating Archie*. By the time I got to writing *Educating Rita* this radio programme was long forgotten, certainly people younger than my generation would never have heard it.
So, I didn't write it with any conscious intention of allusion, in fact I only put it on as a working title. I had to send the script down to Peggy at that time and I couldn't think of a satisfactory title, so I just wrote it as a bit of a joke, that I thought maybe Peggy would get, because she'd know *Educating Archie*. I thought it was a terrible title and my wife, Annie, said it was a wonderful title, why change it? Thank goodness I left it on. Somebody wrote a parody actually and sent it to me a while ago called *Educating Peter*.

2.4 *Educating Rita:* The Stage Play, the Film and the Video

Stage Version

As an introduction to a play reviews are sometimes misleading. They not only depend on the performance itself but also on the audience's reaction and the mood, insight and interests of the reviewer. A critic once suggested to Willy Russell that when Rita gave Frank a haircut it was an allusion to Samson. Russell strenuously denied that such an allusion had ever been intended (see Introduction to Students' Book). But the critic would not change his opinion. The refinements of literary criticism and his own reading of the play were obviously more important to him than what the author had really intended.

Judging from their reviews, Rowena Goldman, Simon Howards and Clive Hirschhorn saw the same production of *Educating Rita* in a slightly different light. Students might like to look closely at the parts of the play referred to by the reviewers and consider to what extent, if at all, the reviewers have read their own interpretations into the play, or whether the text justifies the reviewers' comments. As a follow-up, they can then compare their own impression of the play by noting down the ideas in the reviews they agree and disagree with. They should, perhaps, check that they aren't reading too much into the play themselves.

If the group is sufficiently enterprising to produce a scene from the play on stage or for video, or if they have the chance to see the film or a production of the play, they could write their own reviews for class and group discussion. This would involve them in looking closely at the signals the playwright builds into the dialogue to help the actors translate the play from the page into stage terms.

Review by Simon Howard

Education is what survives when what we have learnt has been forgotten, according to the psychologist B F Skinner.

What might be left, then, for Rita, who learnt nothing at school and claims to remember only broken glass, torn books, knives and fights. And that was just in the staff room.

Now a 26-year-old hairdresser, Willy Russell's heroine is determined to give it another try – to break away from a world where people don't want you to change, where every night is spent, drearily, in the pub. The middle classes would be heartbroken to hear her dismiss local working-class culture as people being "pissed or on valium".

Rita has enlisted on an Open University Literature course and the first of the play's several short scenes brings her before her tutor, Frank. Not a promising start, since he's only doing it to pay for his drinking and anyway complains that the course interferes with pub hours.

In his office, where an empty, fallen bottle lurks behind every book, starts the education of Rita, whose name has been taken from Rita Mae Brown, author of her number one literary enjoyment, *Rubyfruit Jungle*.

"There's less to me than meets the eye," insists Frank. Which isn't entirely true, because he fails to promise much in the first place. But more of that later. He is a one-time author of poems devoted exclusively to his wife who rather obligingly left him so that he might stretch his literary range. Needless to say, he has since abandoned writing.

However, Frank is quite able to appreciate Rita's freshness of approach and realises it will be useless for exam purposes, so he tries to dissuade her from doing the course. But she insists, and is soon bracketing E M Forster with Harold Robbins. (In the post-Blunt era, she's probably not the only one.) An essay question on how to stage *Peer Gynt* is sensibly dealt with: "Do it on the radio."

Of course, the more she attends, the more furious her husband becomes and he takes to burning her Chekhov. He wants her to abandon the course and come off the pill. But the course has come to represent life itself, so she abandons him.

Frank becomes increasingly affected by her visits, cuts down on the drink and precipitates a sort of crisis when he asks her to a dinner party which she fails to attend. Rita is not going to be a court jester to his friends, she tells him. She is in a similarly unhappy halfway position to the hawk in Thom Gunn's *Tamer and Hawk*.

Her first visit to the theatre produces a wonderfully emotional essay that would be quite worthless in an exam. She realises that to go on she will have to be changed.

Time and summer school in London produce from her trendy essays on Blake and an understanding of the classical allusions in Frank's old poems. At last she speaks to the full-time students. Frank, however, has returned to the bottle and has even delivered in lecture form the views on literature that Rita had brought on the first day: "Assonance means getting the rhyme wrong", for example.

She has transformed, but Frank likens her story to *Frankenstein*, not *Pygmalion*. She responds by accusing him of wanting to "keep the natives thick". The whole scheme may be worthless in the end, but she has at least made the choice about her education, and that is the crux of the thing. To her husband, choice meant picking one of eight kinds of lager or deciding between Everton and Liverpool.

Julie Walters's portrayal of Rita was utterly complete on the outside – wonderful nods, precarious balancings on her high heels, ear-piercing squeaks in her voice; producing moments like when, for some reason or other, she couldn't look Frank in the eye. One sometimes felt the inner work was not full, but never mind, it was an outrageous, dazzling performance.

Rita's gains at Frank's expense were echoed in the acting and Mark Kingston usually refused to step out of Julie Walters's shadow. One longed for greater energy in the actor, if not in the character.

Many of his problems came from the writing. As with all of Willy Russell's work, there is an extraordinary imbalance in the quality of the writing. Character often makes way for an idea but, more dangerously, an idea sometimes makes way for an unneccessary quip. One often feels he fails to pay as much attention to his actual writing as to his thinking.

Nevertheless, the thought is important, as are his anger, sense of outrage and compassion. *Educating Rita* is undeniably flawed, but one certainly welcomes its having been written.

(In: *Plays and Players,* June 1980, pp. 19–20.)

Review by Rowena Goldman

The Warehouse is quickly becoming the Hampstead Theatre of the London Fringe – everything the Royal Shakespeare Company touches in this, their other home, seems to turn to gold. The outstanding success of *Piaf* proved this by transferring to the Piccadilly: now Willy Russell's excellent twohander *Educating Rita* has done the same.

This brilliantly performed comedy centres upon the passionate desire of a young Northern girl to attain a proper education in order to equip her for the higher echelons of a life to which she so longingly aspires. Her transformation from a culturally naive modern girl to a successful student is at once subtle and striking in Willy Russell's sharp and witty dialogue and Julie Walters' remarkable performance as Rita. From her first entrance into the study of her prospective tutor, who is to treat her to the delights of an Open University course, she rings true. She wanders wide-eyed around the study, touching the books and announcing that she wants an education, "a better culture". For Frank, the well-worn, quotation-battered intellectual, she is a refreshing change from the pretentious and take-it-or-leave-it attitude of the students he has been used to.

Rita works as a hairdresser and, in her midtwenties, figures that there is more to life than 'creme' rinses and perms that go wrong. She wants to digest Chekhov and Shakespeare, Forster and Ibsen and she wants to pass exams. Frank's prime objective is to draw her away from the trashy paperbacks on which she has been reared and to teach her to appreciate and dissect the qualities of great literature. "How would you solve the problems of staging *Peer Gynt*?" is the title of one essay he sets her. For Rita, unaccustomed as she is to theorizing and churning out facts to please examiners, the answer is simple – "Do it on the radio". Besides coming to grips with the slow learning process, Rita has problems with her husband, whom she tries to convince that an individual has a right to choose. "He thinks we've got choice because we can go into a pub and choose between eight different lagers", and she ends up with, inevitably, a broken marriage but, eventually, an education. Frank, however, does not see this new-found knowledge as a change for the better and in the end there exists between them a relationship not dissimilar to the psychiatrist/patient relationship in *Equus*. He has cured Rita of her so-called ignorance but her passionate innocence has gone. He is left wondering where he will ever find such honesty again and we are left wondering whether Rita, now fully equipped for a better life crammed with opportunities, will find greater happiness. Mark Kingston's portrayal of Frank is a beautiful study of an academic for whom alcohol is an anaesthetic numbing the pain of his failed creativity, and Mike Ockrent's direction of the two performers is well-balanced in this thoroughly entertaining production.

(In: *drama, The Quarterly Theatre Review,* October 1980, pp. 54–55.)

Review by Clive Hirschhorn

To say that Willy Russell's *Educating Rita* (Piccadilly) simply concerns the changes brought about in the life and life-style of a 26-year-old Liverpudlian (Julie Walters) after she acquires some education would hardly do justice, to the richness of the play's writing or the shrewdness of its observations.

On the surface the play is simple enough. Rita, a hairdresser whose husband resents her quest for knowledge, enrols for a year's Open University course. Her tutor (Mark Kingston) is a failed poet called Frank who cauterises the pain of his own unproductive existence by drinking heavily during tutorials.

By contrasting Frank's general disillusionment and boredom with Rita's inarticulate enthusiasm, playwright Russell derives a great deal of humorous mileage, reserving his most poignant moments for the second half in which Rita, having immersed herself in writers like Blake, Wilde, D.H. Lawrence and Chekhov, loses her warmth, spontaneity and freshness.

What we are left with in the end is a woman who, after broadening her mind and "finding" herself, is not nearly as appealing a person as she was just one year earlier.

Directed with total conviction by Mike Ockrent and acted to perfection by its cast of two, *Educating Rita,* is the most enjoyable new British play since *Abigail's Party*. It must be seen.

(From: *Sunday Express,* 24th August 1980)

Film Version

"A play crying out to be made into a film." This was Michael Caine's comment when interviewed on television shortly after the film version of *Educating Rita* appeared, in which he plays Frank and Julie Walters plays Rita. Compared with a stage production, the possibilities a film offers are more varied and flexible. The ideas expressed in the dialogue between Rita and Frank can be spread amongst more characters. In the play, Rita has a number of long speeches. These serve to fill in the background to her life for Frank and the audience, and describe and explain her need to extend her range of experience. She tells of how she and her friends spent their money on records; how they bought new clothes to impress the "fellers" at the clubs – a sort of numbing process to make life bearable. She describes her home background and her life in a working-class area. The camera can move into these streets, homes and pubs which she can only describe in the play.* The cinema-goer is presented with a more immediate and more easily accessible insight into Rita's life and its limitations, making it easier to understand why she felt she had to take an Open University course.

The off-stage characters can appear in the film and speak for themselves. Instead of Rita having to tell Frank about her struggle to make her husband, Denny, understand, we can eavesdrop on their visits to the pub and watch them in their own home. This immediacy helps us to understand Rita's dilemma. Trish and Tiger are two other characters we can see instead of just hearing about. We see at first hand what sort of

* Cf Section E in the interview (16 October 1996), pp. 50.

people they are and what influence they have on Rita. Frank's character is also developed in the film. He is shown in contact with other people apart from Rita both at home and at work. He can be presented as a more rounded character and is not just a sounding board against which Rita, and the audience, can measure her progress. Costume and dress are good guides to character whether in real life or on the stage. On stage, Rita talks a lot about what she is going to wear once she is educated. In the film she dresses in many different ways. From our own observation we can compare Rita's choice of clothes with the way other characters in the film, from the same and different social backgrounds, dress. The film underlines the way her taste in clothes changes as her ideas develop.

When she first appears on the scene, tottering across the quadrangle in her high-heeled shoes, she looks very common. There are pink highlights in her blond peroxide-bleached hair and she is wearing a short, tight skirt and jumper. She looks, and is, completely out of place. We experience her dilemma and the difficulties she has in adjusting to her new social surroundings, by watching her try on one outfit after another to wear at Frank's party. All of them are totally unsuitable. When she moves in with Trish, she tries to imitate her way of dressing, but it is easy to see that it does not fit Rita's character. Slowly, but surely, Rita lets the artificial pink and blond grow out and her natural hair colouring shows through. Parallel to this she begins to find her real self. When she returns from the summer school, there is nothing artificial about her anymore. She no longer tries to create a personality for herself through her choice of clothes. Her dress does not distinguish her in any way from the other students. Her hair is longer and the colour natural. She fits into her surroundings.

The visual presentation of the social and cultural spheres Rita is moving between makes her problems more easily understandable. Despite these problems she makes progress and achieves her aim. The stages of this development are marked by the division of the play into acts and scenes. In the film a leitmotif – a tuneful, easy-to-remember melody – takes over this function. Every time Rita enters into a new phase of her development the melody underlines the action.

The film *Educating Rita* appeared in 1983 and since Willy Russell adapted his own play for the film, it is particularly interesting to compare the stage with the film version. The scene in which Rita tells Frank about her first visit to a professional theatre to see *Macbeth* is a good illustration of his technique. In the play, Rita rushes into Frank's study to tell him how marvellous the production was. A summary of the film sequence of this scene will give a good idea of what is involved in adapting the play for the screen.

In the film, the scene opens with a shot of Rita coming across the university campus in her working clothes. She rushes into the hall and up the stairs.

We are then shown the interior of a groundfloor lecture room with big windows. About twenty students are sitting placidly listening to Frank's lecture on tragedy and taking notes. We hear a few words of the lecture before the scene returns to Rita trying to get into Frank's office. She knocks, struggles with the handle and kicks the bottom of the door. It flies open and Rita bursts into the room. She realizes that Frank is not there and rushes out into the corridor, slamming the door behind her. The scene changes briefly to Frank walking to and fro giving his lecture, before we return to Rita coming down the main staircase, crossing the hall and leaving the building. We return to the lecture room where Frank is still addressing his students. As he speaks we see several of the students looking towards a window. Frank becomes aware of this and follows their look. He sees Rita gesticulating to him excitedly from outside.

With some embarrassment, Frank signals Rita to go round to the entrance of the building. She disappears. He turns to his students with an apology and goes out of the room, leaving the door half open. In the vestibule, Rita hurries eagerly across to Frank and begins to tell him about the performance of *Macbeth* she has seen. Seeing the half-open door, she suddenly realises that she has disturbed Frank but he takes her by the elbow and invites her to hear the rest of the lecture. She is alarmed and resists but Frank leads her into the room and tells the other students that she is a student from another course. Rita sits down and Frank continues his lecture. We have a close shot of Rita glancing nervously about her but as none of the students seem to be interested in her she relaxes and becomes absorbed in what Frank is saying.

Frank: The sort of thing we read in the newspapers as being tragic, "Man Killed By Falling Tree", is not a tragedy.
Close up of Rita as she speaks with utter spontaneity.
Rita: It is for the poor sod under the tree!

The students laugh at her. Frank cuts through the laughter and continues his lecture. The scene is faded out and dissolves to a view of the campus. Groups of students are sitting about the lawn. Rita and Frank are walking and chattering together.

Rita: It's fun tragedy, isn't it?
Frank smiles at her.
Rita: All them ...
She indicates the students.
Rita: ... they know about that sort of thing, don't they?

It is only when Frank invites Rita for lunch that she suddenly remembers her customer at the hairdresser's.

From this summary we can see that the dialogue is pared down to a minimum. The visual elements convey much of the meaning which had to be explicitly expressed in the play. We are shown the university campus which Rita finds so intimidating. We can compare Rita in her working clothes with the students we only hear about in the play. Their calm, academic interest in tragedy, highlights Rita's spontaneous enthusiasm.

Students who have the opportunity to see the film can compare some of the episodes which are related in the play but shown in detail in the film and decide what advantages the film has over the play. Rita is shown at work in the hairdresser's shop dealing with a difficult customer. The family gathering at the pub is shown in detail. It forms a series of flashbacks in Rita's narration to Frank. She explains to him how futile she finds this way of passing the time and how out of place she feels. In the flashbacks we see exactly what she means. At her sister's wedding Rita is shown as an isolated figure, wearing a dress which is totally unsuitable for her. She is not able to join in with the other guests and she is left on her own. Her husband, Denny, deserts her in the middle of a dance. She is equally out of place at Frank's more socially cultivated party. The film shows this scene mainly from Rita's standpoint, outside the house in the rain, in front of an intimidating flight of steps. She does not dare to go up them to the front door into the brightly lit, elegant surroundings and leaves a note under the windscreen wipers of Frank's car. The next flight of steps to Trish's flat she can manage with less trepidation, though the interior was obviously not what she had expected. We also see her in contact with other students at the summer school, joining in conversations on the lawns and earning money for her studies by working in a bistro.

Some scenes are completely new. A new dimension is introduced through the affair between Julia and her best friend's husband, Brian. Brian tries to cover his tracks by picking up the phone and talking to an imaginary publisher whenever Frank comes into the room. One day, however, he finds himself talking into a dead line. Frank has forgotten to pay the phone bill and the line, as he points out to Brian, has been cut off.

Rita's determination and suddenness of decision are shown in a scene in which Denny is renovating their small terrace house. Denny is making two rooms into one and disturbing Rita who is trying to write an essay in the bedroom. When she comes down to see what the noise is about, she finds Denny carefully taking down the wall brick by brick.

She cannot understand why he is being so careful and when he leaves the room, picks up a sledge hammer, squares up to the wall and gives it an almighty blow. The whole top section of the wall comes down with a crash, damaging the main beam supporting the upper floor.

Just before her exams, Rita returns to her old home. She is divorced from Denny and meets him and his new wife, Barbara, who is pregnant. Denny has not changed his views at all and his new wife is very happy with her lot. Rita has chosen another way of life for herself. She no longer fits into Denny's world.

The film also shows Rita visiting Trish in hospital after her suicide attempt. Their conversation puts Rita's search to find her true self in a new light. Rita had envied Trish because she thought she had got everything. She believed Trish unterstood music, painting, literature and poetry. But Trish tells her that these had only been a way of escaping from herself. When the music ends she is confronted with her self and her own life – and life never quite lives up to the promise of the music.

The final scene of the play is also completely new.* Before going to see the film, students could consider how Willy Russell decided to finish the film, where the scene takes place and what it contains. The following synopsis can be used if it is not possible to see the film. The scene is the main concourse of a busy airport. Rita hurries through the crowd towards Passport control where Frank, his hair now short and trim, is about to board the plane to Australia.

Rita has passed her examination. Frank congratulates her and, with sudden warmth, embraces her. The airport official reminds him repeatedly that he must hurry or he will miss his plane. He turns indecisively towards the boarding gate. Rita calls him back to thank him for being such a good teacher. Frank smiles and goes through to board his plane. Rita slowly walks away from the camera down a long deserted corridor. She turns momentarily to look back and then continues decisively on her way and out of our sight.

The film *Educating Rita* can be obtained from Rank Film Library, P.O. Box 70, Great Western Road, Brentford, Middlesex, TW 8 9 HR or from the ELT Verlag, Lederstr. 21, 22525 Hamburg.

A.R.G.

---

* Cf Section D in the Interview (16 October 1996), p. 49.

Video Version*

Educating Rita is an easily accessible play. The dialogue is straightforward and colloquial, the setting is not complicated and the ideas and feelings belong to the world of everyday experience. Short passages taken from the play can easily be prepared for class performance. The same scene can be prepared by several groups, recorded on video and compared by all the members of the class later. This is how one group from a German secondary school set about this task.

"Warum spielt ihr das Stück nicht selbst?"

Meine Frage unterbrach für einen Augenblick die hitzige Diskussion und ließ sie dann um so heftiger wieder aufflammen, bis das dritte Klingeln uns eindringlich aufforderte, an unsere Plätze zurückzukehren. Wir, Leistungskurs Englisch der Jahrgangsstufe 12/2, sahen eine Aufführung der deutschen Fassung von Russells *Educating Rita*, und in der Pause war unter den Schülern eine heftige Diskussion darüber entbrannt, wie weit die deutsche Übersetzung dem Original gerecht wurde und wie weit die Darstellung von Frank und Rita den Vorstellungen der Schüler entsprach.

Kritik wurde insbesondere an der Darstellung des Frank geübt. Die Schüler hatten aufgrund einer voraufgegangenen Unterrichtsreihe nicht nur genaue Textkenntnisse, sondern auch sehr konkrete Vorstellungen von den beiden Charakteren. Als einige Schüler nach der Aufführung in einem Gespräch mit dem Darsteller des Frank mit ihren Einwänden und Fragen überhaupt kein Gehör fanden, war die Entscheidung gefallen: sie wollten versuchen, ihre Vorstellungen von den Rollen in einer Aufführung der Originalfassung zu verwirklichen. Bei soviel Engagement konnte ich als Fachlehrerin nur noch zustimmen – eine neue Arbeitsgemeinschaft war entstanden.

Bei den Vorbesprechungen und den ersten Leseproben schälten sich bald zwei Teams für die Rollen des Zwei-Personen-Stückes heraus. Sehr schnell hatten wir uns auch entschieden, die Komödie auf Video aufzuzeichnen, weil das zum einen für die Darsteller eine gewaltige Arbeitserleichterung bedeutete, da sie ihre Rollen szenenweise lernen konnten (eine weitere Unterteilung ist nicht ratsam, da sonst später sehr viel geschnitten werden muss). Zum anderen können sich die Darsteller nach jeder Szene selbst begutachten und korrigieren, und die Aufzeichnung kann weiterhin für eigene Unterrichtszwecke verwendet werden. Ausschlaggebend war jedoch die Arbeitserleichterung für die Darsteller.

* Cf Select Bibliography (Media), p. 116.

Da das gesamte Stück in dem Raum einer Universität spielt, war es relativ einfach, einen geeigneten Drehort zu finden, nämlich eine Ecke der Schülerbibliothek. Die wichtigsten Requisiten (Bücherregale, Schreibtisch etc.) waren so bereits vorhanden oder leicht zu beschaffen.

Mehr Schwierigkeiten bereitete die Frage, wie Rita und Frank gekleidet sein sollten. Die Bühnenanweisungen gaben hier nur spärliche Auskunft. Wie schon bei der Wahl des Drehortes war auch hier entscheidend, dass die notwendigen Kleidungsstücke ohne allzu großen Aufwand aus eigenen Beständen zu beschaffen waren. Außerdem mussten sie zum Typ des Darstellers passen; deshalb kamen wir z.B. überein, Rita im ersten Akt leger, aber nicht poppig zu kleiden.

Eine weitere wichtige Entscheidung betraf die Sprache. Wir haben darauf verzichtet, Dialekt nachzuahmen. Rita spricht lediglich sehr nachlässig.

Jede dieser Entscheidungen setzte eine intensive Auseinandersetzung mit der Rolle und dem ganzen Stück voraus. Wie betrunken sollte Frank z.B. in Akt II, 3 sein, ohne dass die Szene in bloßen Klamauk ausartete? Sollte Rita in I, 2 mit unbeteiligter Stimme von ihrem bisherigen Alltag erzählen oder eindringlich? Sollte sie wütend, mitfühlend oder verächtlich klingen, wenn sie in I, 4 von der Arbeiterklasse spricht, die spürt, dass sie keine Lebensziele hat und dieses Gefühl der inneren Leere durch Konsum zu ersticken versucht? Andere Entscheidungen bezogen sich auf Mimik oder Gestik. Welche Wirkung wird erzielt, wenn Rita Frank den Rücken zukehrt? Wirkt sie traurig, abweisend oder unbeteiligt? Entspricht das dem Text oder nicht?

Die „Dreharbeiten“ haben für uns alle eine sehr viel intensivere Auseinandersetzung mit dem Text gebracht als sie bei der Lektüre oder auch bei der Interpretation im Unterricht stattfand.

Insbesondere Ritas teils schnoddrige, teils schlagfertige Redeweise hat ihre Spuren bei allen Beteiligten hinterlassen und Anmerkungen wie z.B. “There’s no suppose about it” oder “It’s dead good” oder “You wanna be careful with that stuff, it kills y’ braincells” oder “Don’t be soft” sind inzwischen geläufig. Jener lässige Umgangston, für dieses Stück charakteristisch und den Schülern in ihrer Muttersprache sehr geläufig, wird ansonsten im Sprachunterricht wohl an einzelnen Beispielen vorgeführt, steht den Schülern jedoch nicht aktiv zur Verfügung, wenn sie nicht einige Zeit im englischsprachigen Ausland verbracht haben. Mit dieser Sprachebene vertrauter zu werden und sie selbst der Situation angemessen verwenden zu können, betrachte ich als einen weiteren positiven Aspekt dieser Arbeit.

Der Gewinn und das Vergnügen, das die Dreharbeiten allen bringen, wiegen den Zeitaufwand und die Mühen auf, die mit diesem Projekt verbunden sind.

Ingrid Hartmann-Scheer

3. Integrating the Play into Different Units

Diagram

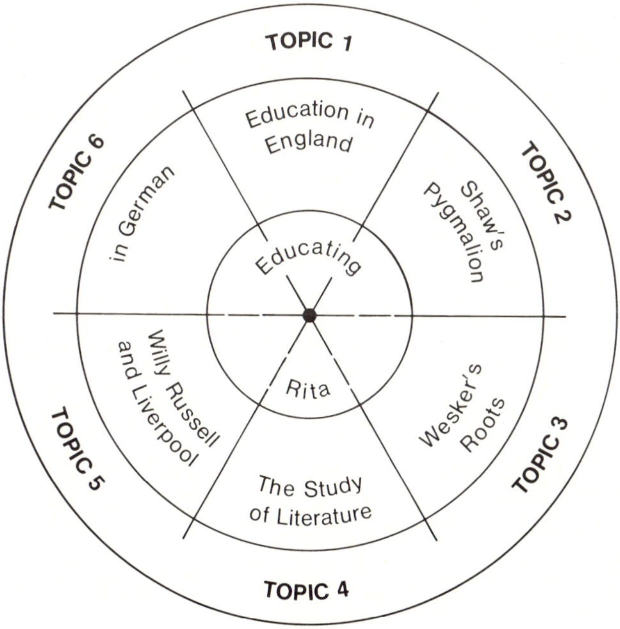

Topics

Topic 1:

Educating Rita and Education in England

Education, at least the school system, in England and/or the USA is part and parcel of the syllabuses for secondary schools in the Federal Republic of Germany. In some Bundesländer it is even obligatory for English classes in the Sekundarstufe II (cf. Nordrhein-Westfalen. Richtlinien für die gymnasiale Oberstufe. Englisch. Köln: Greven, 1981, p. 56). *Educa-*

ting Rita could be at the centre of a thematic unit. The Students' Book contains both non-fictional and fictional texts for accompanying work. If a more detailed description of the Open University is required in the course, the texts on pp. 85–92 in the Students' Book can be starting points for a more thorough discussion.

In Act I, Scene 8 of *Educating Rita* (p. 51) Rita tells Frank that her husband has deliverd her an ultimatum: "He said either I stop comin' here an' come off the pill or I could get out altogether." And Rita goes on to quote Denny: "He says there's a time for education. An' it's not when y' twenty-six an' married." Denny thinks that Rita should be committed to the norm of marriage. Rita, however, believes that women should not be conditioned to confine their aspirations to the role of wife/mother. At least she wants to discover herself first and find a better way of living her life: "See, I don't wanna baby yet. See, I wanna discover meself first" (Act I, Scene 1, p. 18).

The interpretation of *Educating Rita* as a central text in a thematic unit can also lead on to a discussion of other important aspects of the English educational system, such as the Public School, the Comprehensive School System, streaming and examinations.

The 'Select Bibliography' at the end of this book lists some useful publications for further studies in these fields. Fictional texts on some of the aspects mentioned are to be found in the Students' Book (pp. 117–135). They can also familiarize the students with some of the differences between education in the past and in the present. The beginning of *Hard Times* (1854), a novel by Charles Dickens, for instance, can initiate a discussion on the problems and functions of acquiring factual knowledge. The scene is an imaginary industrial town called Coketown. One of the main characters is Thomas Gradgrind, an educationist, who believes that education should be merely practical and hence factual, allowing no place for imagination or emotion. The excerpt from *Tom Brown's School Days* (1857) can be contrasted with the previous passage. Whereas Dickens criticized education, Hughes pointed to what seemed to him to be the best aspects of the English school tradition. He sets his story in an English public school. The young boys have been sent to Rugby to become – as Tom's father says – "brave, helpful, truth-telling gentlemen, and Christians".

The passage from *Kes* (1968) by Barry Hines, to give one more example, throws some light on the teacher-pupil-relationship and the conflicts arising out of it. A school edition (with Teacher's Book) of *Kes* is available (Berlin: Cornelsen).

The different aspects of English education have been dramatized by various contemporary playwrights. It would certainly be worthwhile comparing and contrasting scenes from these plays with scenes from *Educating Rita*. Moreover, scenes from the plays can be used to complement the discussion of Russell's play by drawing the students' attention to topics not dealt with in *Educating Rita*. The following brief summaries may serve as an introductory orientation.

Other Plays on Education

Mary O'Malley: *Once a Catholic* (1978)
"A marvellous, irreverent, affectionate and warmly comic play about the confusions and contradictions and general awfulness of being a Catholic schoolgirl."

Simon Gray: *Quartermaine's Terms* (1981)
"Set in the 1960's in a school teaching English to foreigners, Simon Gray's play follows the varying fortunes of the school and its staff-particularly of St. John Quartermaine ..."

Julian Mitchell: *Another Country* (1982)
"*Another Country* is set in an English public school in the early 1930's. The future leaders of the English ruling class are being prepared for their roles in the Establishment. But the two central characters are outsiders: Guy Bennett, coming to terms with homosexuality, and Tommy Judd, a committed Marxist. Judd wants to abolish the whole system of British life; Bennett wants a successful career within it but school, and the system, have traditional ways of dealing with rebels."

Ted Whitehead: *The Punishment* (1976)
"The boy, Anthony, has been recalled from his vacation by the Headmaster, a daunting figure made more awesome by the authority vested in him by the Church – Anthony has offended. His educational future is in the balance. He accepts without question that he must expiate his sin by submitting to corporal punishment."

James Saunders: *The Pedagogue.* A Monodrama (1968)
"*The Pedagogue* is a monologue by a schoolmaster which brilliantly combines the most observation with the most profound illumination of the human condition."

(The quotations listed above are taken from the respective editions of the plays, i.e. back covers, front flaps, etc.; cf. bibliography.)

Topic 2

Educating Rita and Shaw's *Pygmalion**

Educating Rita is a two-hander, a play with two characters, consisting of two acts with a dividing line in the middle. *Pygmalion* is a full-blown five-act work with a turning-point between Acts III and IV. In terms of structure, the two plays do not seem to have a great deal in common. But a closer look at the ideas, the characters and the language of the two plays reveals not only differences but many areas of comparison and counterpoint.

The authors of both plays are no strangers to the implications and pitfalls of giving an essentially middle-class education to children from working-class backgrounds. Shaw came from a poor family. He learned nothing at the various schools he attended, but educated himself by reading Dickens, Shakespeare, Bunyan, and the Bible. At the age of fifteen he obtained a position as clerk in a firm of land agents, his salary being four shillings a week. Willy Russell describes himself as coming from the working class. He left school at 15 and after trying his hand at several unskilled jobs, decided to train to be a teacher.

Topic – Context – Sources

Shaw drew his inspiration from Ovid's *Metamorphoses*. In the legend, a mythological Greek sculptor falls in love with the statue of a woman that he has carved out of ivory, and incites Venus to bring the figure to life so that he can marry the woman. Shaw reverses this process. In *Pygmalion* Higgins takes a live girl, Eliza, and, in the course of Acts II and III, turns her into a work of art. During Acts IV and V this artistic creation assumes life and freedom. The real climax comes in Act V when Eliza accepts and asserts her new identity.

A similar process is also evident in Rita's education and she, too, is bound up in the reversal of a "legend". In Rita's case it is the legend of Frankenstein. Russell's comedy is a continuation and a reversal of Shaw's *Pygmalion*. The cockney-speaking flower girl from Covent Garden is replaced by a working-class girl from the north of England, who speaks Scouse. Higgins discovers Eliza and by means of constant schooling and bullying tries to make her speech presentable. Rita discovers herself and wishes to improve the quality of her life by studying literature. Frank is

* Cf Section C in the Interview (October 16th, 1996), pp. 47–48.

an anti-Pygmalion, a new Mary Shelley (as he likes to call himself at the end) because like her, he feels that he, too, has created a Frankenstein.

Main Characters: Similarities and Differences

Despite some differences, Eliza and Rita, the main characters in the two plays, have much in common. Both are open-minded, spontaneous and honest, and both want to make headway and progress in the world. The most striking similarity is in their speech. When they first appear on stage they both speak dialect; Rita in Scouse, Eliza in Cockney. Eliza has to learn how to avoid the "glottal stop", i.e. to pronounce the /h/ sound properly, especially in initial position, which is not a feature of the Cockney dialect. Eliza is not familiar either with the correct pronunciation of certain vowels and diphthongs.

The Flower girl:
(Eliza) Ow, eez yə-ooa san, is e? Wal, fewd dan y' də-ooty bawmz a mather should, eed now bettern to spawl a pore gel's flahrzn than ran awy athaht pyin. Will ye-oo py me f'them? (*Pygmalion*, p. 16)

Rita is more fortunate in this respect. Frank implores her to use her own natural accent and even allows himself to be influenced by her way of speaking. When drunk, Frank falls off the rostrum twice during a lecture.

Rita: Frank, you're mad.
Frank: Completely off my cake. I know …
Assonance – I said to them – Assonance means getting the rhyme wrong (p. 66).

Higgins equates fine speech and manners with cultured society. Frank sees down-to-earth truths reflected in Rita's speech and remains blind to its limitations. Higgins uses Eliza as an experiment in phonetics. He accepts a wager that he can change a flower girl into a lady simply by changing her speech. He sets about his task in a restlessly analytical and scientific manner disregarding, even dismissing, Eliza's feelings. Frank is horrified at the change he is creating in his pupil. The aspect of Rita's character which his teaching is helping to develop seems in danger of swamping the Rita he loves.

Frank is not beyond wanting to show off his student just as shamelessly as Higgins. He invites Rita and her husband, Denny, to dinner and is annoyed that Rita stays away because she feels the other guests would patronize her and laugh at her as though she were a court jester. Rita and Eliza feel uncomfortable in their new social surroundings. Rita's first problem is what to wear. She worries about what she can talk about, buys the wrong wine, gets on the wrong bus and arrives late. Finally her courage fails her and she goes home.

The inner transformation of Eliza and Rita is mirrored in the change in their outward appearance. In both plays there are allusions to conventions in dress. The same is true of their teachers, Professor Higgins and Frank, who also have traits of character in common. They are apt to lose their self-control, Frank especially, when aroused by feelings of jealousy. On a deeper level they both experience bitter disappointment at their students leaving them. This emancipation attained by both students through means of education is the basic thing the two plays have in common.

But whereas Frank's interest in Rita is not confined to teaching her literature, Higgins is solely interested in Eliza as a scientific experiment, and only later on develops feelings of love and affection for her. Although he tries to conceal his emotional involvement, Frank's feelings for Rita break out. He is intensively jealous of Rita's friend and fellow student, "Mr-Tiger-Tyson", and of his proposed trip to the south of France. He regrets that he has been so successful in educating Rita, which Higgins could never bring himself to admit.

Frank: Oh I've done a fine job on you, haven't I.
Rita: It's true, Frank. I can see now.
Frank: You know, Rita, I think – I think that like you I shall change my name; from now on I shall insist upon being known as Mary, Mary Shelley – do you understand that allusion, Rita?
Rita: What?
Frank: She wrote a little Gothic number called *Frankenstein*.

Rita does not understand the allusion but her common sense gives her a very clear idea of what Frank is suffering.

Rita: I'll tell you what you can't bear, Mr Self-Pitying Piss Artist; what you can't bear is that I am educated now. (p. 73)

The academic smugness exhibited by both teachers leads to their downfall. In the course of the plays they have to relinquish the role of dominator and change places with their pupils. The naturally stronger and more spontaneous characters of Rita and Eliza take control. Higgins does not merely make Eliza's speech more ladylike. At the end of the experiment she decides to do without him, chooses a life style on a different social level and marries Freddy. Rita also learns that choice is a precious commodity. The personal situation between her and Frank is reversed. In the beginning, Frank is Rita's only glimmer of hope. In the end, she is the only living being in his otherwise arid environment, and she is even obliged to break with him. He has been a good teacher to Rita; too good for his own peace of mind: "I don't need you. I've got a room full of books. I know what clothes to wear, what wine to buy, what plays to see, what papers and books to read. I can do without you." (p. 74)

Rita and Eliza learn that they can choose for themselves, that they do not have to be bound by the ideas other people have of them.

Frank: What are you going to do?
Rita: I dunno. I might go to France. I might go to me mother's. I might even have a baby. I dunno. I'll make a decision, I'll choose. I dunno. (p. 77)

Frank's own estimation of himself is that he is another Mary Shelley. He wants to start a new life and leaves for Australia. Higgins, on the other hand, does not change in the course of the play.

Other Characters: Functions and Language

A closer look at the other characters in both plays reveals a mixture of similarities and differences. Rita's mother, a representative of the working class, can be compared with Eliza's father, Mr Doolittle. Unlike him, however, she is dissatisfied with her social status and wants to "sing a better song", in other words, to climb the social ladder. Both Rita's mother and Alfred Doolittle put their stamp on their daughters, though in different ways. Rita does not want to be a hairdresser any more, whereas Eliza remains keen on selling flowers but in "a more educated way".

Trish has an important function in the play. Although she remains an offstage character, never once appearing before the audience, her influence on Rita is strong and can be detected. In *Pygmalion* there are several characters who share this function. Clara, Mrs Higgins, Mrs Pearce and Colonel Pickering, all try to assist Eliza. Trish and Pickering are the catalysts and the principal mediators in the respective plays.

Mrs Pearce and Trish have similar functions. They are the first to accept and promote the protégées seriously in their new roles. Freddy and Tiger are representatives of the area of society Rita and Eliza are trying to enter, and their friendships mark the acceptance of the "heroines" into these social strata.

Mr Doolittle and Pickering, despite their many differences, both bring a breath of everyday realism on to the stage. This function is performed by reference to offstage characters in *Educating Rita*.

Despite his opinion of himself, there is an emotional side to Frank's nature which Higgins lacks. Frank did, after all, once write poetry. In *Pygmalion* Pickering portrays this side of human nature. The easy-going, retired, ex-Indian army-officer serves as a contrast to his scientifically-minded friend and brings an element of real artistic appreciation, creative sensitivity and cultured behaviour into the play.

Although its background is phonetics the basic theme of *Pygmalion* is human relations. The characters are strongly portrayed and each person's character is mirrored in his speech. Higgins uses the robust and energetic scientific language of the expert. His friend, Colonel Pickering's speech is better modulated and more refined, as is his character. Alfred Doolittle, Eliza's father, is an elderly and rigorous man with speech patterns as eccentric and forthright as his opinions and behaviour. The professor's mother, Mrs Higgins, is an equally determined parent, but a pleasant woman who, for all her determination, expresses herself pleasantly.

Not unlike Eliza, Rita marks her passage from one intellectual sphere to another by going through a phase of talking in a stilted and unnatural way. But whereas Frank wants Rita to stay the way she has always been, Higgins wants to change Eliza's way of speaking. He teaches her to speak with pedantic correctness. Rita tries to impose this restraint on herself. In Act II, Scene 2, Rita begins to talk in a peculiar voice.

Frank: ... What's wrong with your voice?
Rita: Nothing is wrong with it, Frank. I have merely decided to talk properly. (p. 62)

And she refers to Trish.

Rita: As Trish says there is not a lot of point in discussing beautiful literature in an ugly voice.
Frank: You haven't got an ugly voice; at least you *didn't* have. Talk properly. (p. 62)

A.R.G.

Pygmalion revisited with a scouse accent

By Geoffrey Hutton

There is always something new coming from the Merseyside.

Willy Russell has little in common with The Beatles except that he has the Lancashire flavor and his musical play about them became a London hit.

So much so that the Royal Shakespeare Company commissioned this play which set records in the West End.

Not surprisingly either, because this is a funny, intensely human play which never sags, never lapses into farce and rings as true as a bell. The records it set at the Piccadilly Theatre in London were no fluke.

The Rita of the title is an undereducated Lancashire housewife who aspires to higher things than life with the family or with her uninteresting husband.

Like many other young English people with an ambition to learn she joins the Open University which gives part-time courses to working people.

The parallel with Shaw's *Pygmalion* is obvious.

Rita's ambition is not to learn how to talk like the toffs, she wants to learn about English literature.

Nor is Frank, the tutor, a Professor Higgins, he is a university teacher with a deep sense of despair about his failure to become a poet, who takes his consolation from whisky.

Unlike *Pygmalion,* Russell's play is not about the relationship of phonetics to social status. He is writing about people and digs much deeper into human nature than the old propagandist.

We watch the academic failure gradually sink into alcoholism, (he is finally sent to Australia for two years, which he considers hardly better than being sacked).

At the same time Rita, after a mocking example of talking posh, takes over as the educator. With a fresh mind she has absorbed what was on offer, with a jaded mind he has lost it.

Like Shaw in the original, Russell has steered away from a romantic conclusion – it would seem too sentimental – so he ends with a nice, unexpected joke.

Willy Russell is one of a new wave of English playwrights, and I would pick him as a stayer, like John Osborne in the 1950s and '60s. His subject is topical, his dialogue lively, and he writes for an audience, not for his own urge for self-expression.

The play was given its Australian premiere in Perth, and Julia Moody was chosen for the title role by the author after she had completed a course at the Bristol Old Vic Theatre School.

It is hard to imagine anybody playing it better. The accent comes naturally and easily: she is intensely alive and responsive to mood, varying from scene to scene and moving from nervous clumsiness to cool self-confidence.

Andy King, as the tutor, opens as first fiddle, and moves naturally to the second desk, in all ways a very adequate and effective foil, grumpy at times, blustering occasionally, but always on the beat.

The play has been re-staged by Ray Lawler and designed by Mark Wager with a complicated lighting pattern by Jamie Lewis.

(From: *The Australian*, 23 April 1983)

For Classroom Work

The two plays *Educating Rita* and *Pygmalion** can be compared and contrasted in terms of

- their characters:
  character traits, development, dilemmas at the end of the play.
- the teachers' attitudes to their respective students, to changing their students.
- the language of the two protagonists.

The characters

Age, origin, profession, marital status

Eliza	Rita
• Age 18-20 • lower class, East London • flower girl • Cockney accent • single	• Age 26 • working-class, Liverpool • hairdresser • Scouse • married

Character traits

Eliza	Rita
• bright, spontaneous, outspoken • wants to "talk more genteel" so as to get ahead (flower shop) • innocent, charming	• bright, outspoken, spontaneous • hungry for knowledge • innocent, charming

Development

• **I:** from flower girl to society lady • **II:** from society lady ("speaking doll") to a vivacious woman who asserts her new identity	• from hairdresser to university graduate • from innocence to experience • from the trap of her working-class milieu to choice given to her by her education

Dilemmas

• New language, manners, refinement make it impossible for her to return to her old job. • Higgins' education limits her opportunities. → **II & III:** A flower girl is made into an artificial duchess by the skill of an expert. → "Whats to become of me?" (75) "Now youve made a lady of me I'm not fit to sell anything else. I wish youd left me where you found me." (77)	• O.U. education cuts her off from her husband and family. "I can't talk to the people I live with anymore. … I'm a half-caste." (50)
However:	However:
• Higgins' insensitive treatment arouses resentment in Eliza: → **IV & V:** The speaking doll becomes a live woman, her own vitality/identity asserts itself: Eliza chooses to leave Higgins and marry Freddy! "But I can do without you: dont think I cant." (98)	• Frank's education gives Rita 'choice': "I might go to France. I might go to me mother's. I might even have a baby. I dunno. I'll make a decision. I'll choose." (77)

Scenes that lend themselves to comparison in the two plays

Pygmalion	Educating Rita
• pp. 21-25 (II) Higgins meets the flowergirl.	• pp. 7-15 (I.1) Rita entering Frank's room.
• pp.57-62 (III) Higgins introduces Eliza to his mother.	• pp. 48-51 (I.7) Rita is invited to Frank's place.
• pp.103-107 (IV) Scene with slippers.	• pp. 73-76 (II.5) "Why don't you go away."
• pp. 134-136 Epilogue.	• p. 77 (II.7) Rita thanks Frank. Rita has "choice".

The teachers' attitudes to their respective students, to changing their students

Higgins' attitude to Eliza	Frank's attitude to Rita
• Very condescending ("baggage", "So deliciously low, so horribly dirty", 26), contemptuous • Is very rude to her. • Bosses her about. • Treats her as if she were a servant.	• Admires her, is charmed by her spontaneity, likes her frankness.
• Sees it as a challenge to educate her. • Does not value her abilities highly: "She's incapable of understanding anything." (31) • Not worried about the consequences his education will have on Eliza. • Being a bachelor, having a professional code of honour he guarantees Eliza's safety. Higgins is a man of good character.	• Does not want to teach her, is worried he might kill her spontaneity/uniqueness. • Frank is worried about the consequences his education will have on Rita. • Frank fancies Rita, makes various attempts to get close to her (invitation to his house, jealous of Tiger-Tyson, Blake poem and his squeamishness about its sexual references).

Gunther Volk

* All page references are to the Longman Literature Edition (1991) of *Pygmalion*.

Topic 3

Educating Rita and Wesker's *Roots*

Roots (1958) is the middle part of the so-called Wesker Trilogy, the other two plays being *Chicken Soup with Barley* (1958) and *I'm Talking about Jerusalem* (1960). The central characters in *Chicken Soup with Barley* are the members of the Kahn family. They are Jewish communists living in London between 1936 and 1956. Ronnie Kahn can, to a certain extent, be identified with Wesker. He is disillusioned with the communist ideals.

In *Roots* we meet Ronnie Kahn only through the medium of his girlfriend, Beatie Bryant. He does not appear in the play. The place of action is a cottage in Norfolk, the house of the Bealeses. Jenny Beales is Beatie Bryant's sister. The world of *Roots* is completely rural. Beatie has come back to her family in Norfolk for a holiday. She is expecting Ronnie to join her.

The following extract from Glenda Leeming's book *Wesker the Playwright* encapsulates what *Roots* is about:

> Nothing much happens, except that we see Beatie's suppressed unease about the gap between Ronnie's intellectual, political and cultural interests, and her own limited horizons (and unwillingness to extend them). These qualities are shared by her family. Then, dramatically, as the whole family is assembled to meet Ronnie, a letter arrives from him instead, jilting Beatie. This shock provokes Beatie into a painful reassessment of herself and her assumptions, and into the very awareness and articulacy that Ronnie has despaired of her ever finding. Blackly ironic from Beatie's point of view, her breakthrough into being 'articulate at last' makes for an upbeat ending. Ronnie's determination to 'save someone from the fire', seemingly doomed by Beatie's stolid materialism, is suddenly seen to be justified. People can change for the better. Environmental influences can be counteracted. Beatie *can* grow roots.
>
> (London: Methuen 1983, p. 44)

Beatie and her Family

In contrast to Rita who realizes herself that the life she has been living does not satisfy her anymore, it is only through Ronnie that Beatie Bryant becomes aware of the fact that life should be more than commonplace and daily routine. Beatie comes from a family of farm labourers. She is a waitress in a London hotel. There she met Ronnie Kahn who has been her friend for three years and whose political and cultural ideas have made a strong impression on her. When coming home for a holiday,

Beatie makes attempts to familiarize her family with her new ideas. She tries to convey her 'message' about what life should also be:

Beatie: [...] it's living, it's singing, it's dancing, it's being interested in what goes on around you, it's being concerned about the people and the world. (p. 129)

But the family are closed to new ideas, they are incapable of exchanging ideas. They don't even chat much. When Jenny and Jimmy Beales converse, (not really: communicate) with each other, they do so in three-or-four-word sentences most of the time. "They talk in fits and starts mainly as a sort of gossip, and they talk quickly too, enacting as though for an audience what they say. Their sense of humour is keen and dry [...]" (stage direction, p. 92).

Beatie and Rita

Beatie and Rita have many things in common. Both are young: Rita is 26, Beatie 22 years of age. Both are members of the lower working class. But whereas Rita was brought up near a big industrial town, Liverpool, Beatie's family are country people in Norfolk. The two characters suffer from their deficient education. So far they have not been given a chance to work for higher degrees and thereby qualify for better jobs and higher social positions. Thus Rita has become a hairdresser, and Beatie works as a waitress in a London hotel to make a living. Rita is married to Denny who wants a child and expects her to play the role that tradition and conventions ascribe to the woman.

Both Rita and Beatie start emancipating themselves from their social surroundings. Rita takes an Open University course, passes her exams and ends up as an educated and emancipated person. Denny objects fiercely to Rita's new ideas, he burns her books and finally sends her away. He does not understand Rita's change of mind.

Things are different with Ronnie, Beatie's friend. He tries to talk Beatie into changing her life, he encourages her to break out of her rural defeatism. Ronnie is superior to Beatie, culturally and educationally. He is keen on and capable of giving her an insight into what higher education has to offer. He explains to her what culture really means, why classical music is of greater value than popsongs, why skimming comics cannot really be a substitute for reading the *Manchester Guardian*.

As far as Beatie and Rita themselves are concerned, there seems to be one important difference. Beatie gets involved with education primarily because she loves Ronnie. She even admits that in the beginning she pretended to be interested in what he had to say because she did not want to lose him. Rita, on the other hand, took the Open University course for the sole purpose of acquiring more education. From the very start she made it a point that love should be left out.

Both Rita and Beatie are separated from their partners eventually. The question whether Rita's friendship with Tiger will develop into a new permanent relationship is left open in *Educating Rita*. Both leave their families behind. In the end Rita and Beatie are "educated" and independent. Rita puts it this way, when talking to her tutor: "I'm educated, I've got what you have an' y' don't like it because you'd rather see me as the peasant I once was; you're like the rest of them – you like to keep your natives thick, because that way they still look charming and delightful. I don't need you". (p. 75)

Beatie who, in the course of the play, has parroted Ronnie's opinions without really grasping them, finally understands what Ronnie has been trying to convey. The uncompromising and stolid reactions of the different members of her family finally result in Beatie's trying to fulfil Ronnie's demands and make her ideas materialize in her own life. As Ronald Hayman (*British Theatre since 1955. A Reassessment*, p. 45) puts it:

> ... it is only at the end of the play that argument and action are triumphantly welded together as Beatie, who has been jilted by Ronnie, finds out by talking that she is no longer parroting his opinions. She has made them into her own.

Comparing and Contrasting the two Plays

Unlike *Educating Rita, Roots* is not a comedy. The play consists of three acts, whereas Russell's play has a two-act-structure with a clear-cut dividing line between the two parts. *Educating Rita,* as a stage play, is a two-hander. Only Frank and Rita appear on stage, they make, however, references to some off-stage characters, who constitute the background. In Wesker's *Roots*, it is Ronnie Kahn who does not make an appearance, he is a kind of catalyst gearing the action from the outside. The action in *Roots* takes place within two weeks in which Beatie loses her friend and finds herself. *Educating Rita* takes place in a first-floor room in a university in the north of England. Here the action stretches over a much longer period of time including Rita's going to a summer school in London. Both plays contain elements of regional varieties of the English language. In *Roots* it is the dialect of the rural people in Norfolk. Some of its characteristics are described by Arnold Wesker (*The Wesker Trilogy*, London 1966, p. 83):

Double 'ee' is pronounced 'i' as in 'it' – so that 'been' becomes 'bin', 'seen' becomes 'sin' etc. 'Have' and 'had' become 'hev' and 'hed' as in 'head' ... Instead of the word 'of' they say 'on', e. g. 'I've hed enough on it' or 'What do you think on it?'.

This dialect, similar to the Liverpudlian Scouse in *Educating Rita,* has a functional meaning in the play, in the sense that it is an integral part of the portrayal of some of the characters.

For Classroom Work

Testing the Understanding of 'Roots' and 'Educating Rita'

After an interpretation and discussion of *Roots* with students in a 'Leistungskurs 12/1' an extract from *Educating Rita* (pp. 38–40) was given to the students with the tasks listed below:

- Sum up briefly what happened between Rita and her husband Denny before Rita comes to this tutorial.
- Why do Rita and Denny quarrel?
- What does the playwright achieve by making Rita tell Frank about the row she had with her husband instead of showing Rita and Denny quarrelling on stage?
- Compare Rita as she is presented in this passage with Beatie Bryant. In which respect are they similar or different?

As Russell's play was unknown to the students, a few vocabulary aids (e.g. *shack up with; Peer Gynt; lager; Everton; dole*) and the following brief introduction were added to the extract:

> Rita, a 26-year-old hairdresser, has decided to take an Open University course in English literature. Her tutor is Frank, who teaches literature at the university.

With reference to a comparison between *Educating Rita* and *Roots*, the last of the four tasks is of special interest.

Below are examples of how two students tackled the task in different ways. The first essay was submitted by an exchange student from the USA in the class (I), the second being submitted by a German student (II). No alterations whatsoever were undertaken for publication purposes. This applies to both content and language.

I am most grateful to Ingrid Hartmann-Scheer of the Theodor-Heuss-Schule in Ratingen for giving me permission to publish the material in this book.

I.

The most obvious similarities between Rita and Beatie are in their upbringing in a home opposed or indifferent to education (in Rita's case it is assumed) and the ensuing inner conflict and outward struggle for acceptance. Both women have come to know the glories of education later in life than is usually expected, and both are isolated in their discoveries. Both women are struggling to find acceptance among family members, and perhaps even to share their discoveries. Both are faced with the obstacle of trying to reach people unwilling or unable to understand. They both are striving to find ways to express themselves, and both seem to meet, and overcome, a great deal of frustration.

Beatie seems to be more certain of herself, and she finds the means of expressing herself by quoting Ronnie. Rita, on the other hand, seems less certain of herself and the justification of her actions. She has no one to quote, except perhaps Frank, but it is unlikely she would quote him while talking to him. This may also be a factor in her trouble expressing herself, but it is not probable.

Beatie, at times, seems less sincere about her education than Rita does. While Rita wants to forgo having children for a while, Beatie seems to consider motherhood as an excuse to stop learning. Rita does not show signs of an inability to understand the material in her course, while Beatie admits that sometimes she does not understand what Ronnie's friends are talking about but neither will she ask them to explain.

Beatie is also quick to place much of the blame of her unenlightened rearing on her mother, while Rita does not actually place the blame on anyone, but seems to blame herself in a way for wanting to become educated and in the process upsetting the relationship she has with Denny.

Of course, because Beatie is more developed than Rita is here in this excerpt, one can easily contrast Beatie's vices to Rita's virtues. In this text Rita is presented as a person struggling in a situation. The playwright wants to show his struggle, and its virtues, so he is unlikely to point out any of her vices in this scene.

Both women, however, are virtuous in their pursuit for education. Rita seems to be more virtuous because she does it mainly for self-enlightenment – as a provision for life itself, while Beatie's initial motives were to catch a husband. The conflict in Rita's case comes from the disruption of her married life and her feelings of guilt. Both women overcome their conflicts.

In Beatie's case she realizes that there is something beyond education than catching a husband and she is then able to express herself. The realization and the ability to express come almost simultaneously at the end of the play after she finds out that Ronnie is not coming to her parents' home. For Rita, she realizes that she must not blame herself for learning or for changing. She sees this when she says, "Well, if he doesn't want me when I'm alive I'm certainly not just gonna lie down an' die for him." (p. 40)

Both playwrights seem to be expressing the virtues of education. They seem to bear a message that it is never too late to learn, but that it becomes harder to become socially accepted as one grows older and becomes set in a certain social class. Although it is not certain in the excerpt about Rita, it is likely that both plays are also aimed at the educated class, to take a look at what they have got, to appreciate it, and not to lose or abuse it. This possibility is hinted at in the following lines:

Rita: ... I told him I'd only have a baby when I had choice. But he doesn't understand. He thinks we've got choice because we can go into a pub that sells eight different kinds of lager. He thinks we've got choice already: choice between Everton an' Liverpool, choosin' which washin' powder, choosin' between one lousy school an' the next, between lousy jobs or the dole ... (p. 40),

where Rita begins to lament the fact that there really are no choices for the uneducated person.

II.

I think there is one basic similarity between Beatie Bryant and Rita. This similarity lies in their behaviour. They are both very outspoken and able to defend their opinions against others, Beatie against her family, Rita against Denny. They've both started emancipating from their actual social surroundings, they've both got in contact with education and educated people, they're both learning and they're both offered a new life based on more education.

But in my opinion the reason and way of both's approach to education is quite different. Beatie got into contact with education only because she fell in love with Ronnie. For her he was different from others because he was intellectual, educated and a socialist. But the only important point is that she really loves him and therefore she doesn't care for the fact that she hasn't got much in common with him and how difficult it'll be for her – "uneducated" as she is – to live with an educated man. She admits that she only pretended to be interested in what he told her just in order not to lose him. Rita's way of approach is just the other way round. She intends from the beginning to get education and her approach is not a private one like Beatie's but an official one: she actually takes an Open University course for the only purpose of getting education. And in addition to that she makes clear – absolutely, in contrast to Beatie – that she wants to keep love away from this. ("I'm busy enough findin' meself, let alone findin' somebody else. I don't want anyone else".) (p. 38)

It becomes obvious that education for Beatie is, from the beginning, connected with Ronnie's person, but for Rita it is connected just with herself: "All I want for the time bein' is what I'm findin' inside me." (p. 38) But there is one thing they have in common in the long run. For both of them education becomes something that is "providin' me with life itself" as Rita says in this extract (p. 39) and which you can also find in *Roots*, when Beatie wants her family to become alive, to get out of their passivity. This aspect of education making one take part in life, keeping one alive appears in both: Beatie and Rita. Beatie has not noticed her being uneducated before meeting Ronnie. She has got many difficulties with education and refuses – as she finally admits – making stronger efforts before Ronnie's letter arrives and she manages to become fully independent. Rita on the other hand is from the beginning full of willpower to make her way to being educated and concentrates fully on this purpose leaving out everything else.

Topic 4

Educating Rita and the Study of Literature

After an interpretation of *Educating Rita* the aims and ways of approaching literary texts could be made a point of discussion. There are always students who find it difficult to interpret poems and other pieces of literature. There are others who object to what they consider to be a dissection of literature. The two extremes of dealing with literary texts are "partisan interpretation", i.e. a spontaneous, subjective, uncritical appreciation on the one hand, and criticism which does not allow either sentimentality or subjectivity but must be "supported by reference to established literary critique" (Frank) on the other hand. Rita's problems and difficulties when approaching literature may also apply to some students in the course. Why not have them slip into Rita's role and tackle some of the literary texts that Rita had to interpret or write essays on, Blake's poem, for instance ("O Rose, thou art sick!"), or an extract from

Howards End by E. M. Forster (a Penguin edition of the novel is available, No. 311).

Act I, Scene 6 of *Educating Rita* with its references to Shakespeare's *Macbeth* will be seen in a different light once the students have ploughed their way through the script of the play.

"And who are you citing in support of your thesis, F. R. Leavis?" (Frank, p. 25) Side by side with this question the students may consider the following paragraph by F. R. Leavis, the famous literary critic. He is discussing an American critic's belief that the intention of Henry James in his novels was closely bound up with a certain philosophical system, that in fact the writing of the novels depended largely on the author's having adopted that system:

F. R. Leavis, The Common Pursuit

But what I have to insist on is that intention in the important sense can only be determined by the tests applied in literary criticism. The analysis and judgement of works of literary art belong to the literary critic, who *is* one in so far as he observes a disciplined relevance in response, comment and determination of significance. He is concerned with the work in front of him as something that should contain within itself the reason why it is so and not otherwise. The more experience – experience of life and literature together – he brings to bear on it the better, of course; and it is true that extraneous information may make him more percipient. But the business of critical intelligence will remain what it was: to ensure relevance of response and to determine what is actually *there* in the work of art. The critic will be especially wary how he uses extraneous knowledge about the writer's intentions. Intentions are nothing in art except as realized, and the tests of realization will remain what they were. They are applied in the operation of the critic's sensibility; they are a matter of his sense, derived from his literary experience, of what the living thing feels like – of the difference between that which has been willed and put there, or represents no profound integration, and that which grows from a deep centre of life. These tests may very well reveal that the deep animating intention (if that is the right word) is something very different from the intention the author would declare.

(London: Chatto & Windus 1965, pp. 224–225)

Topic 5

Willy Russell and Liverpool*

Willy Russell writes about the people of his home city, Liverpool. This does not only apply to *Educating Rita*, and his new musical *Blood Brothers*, but also to his TV plays *The Boy with the Transistor Radio* (In: Self, David (ed.), *Working*. London: Hutchinson 1980, pp. 25–48) and *Our Day Out* (In: Self, David/Speakman, Ray (eds.), *Act One*. London: Hutchinson 1979, pp. 75–137) which are worthwhile discussing in the classroom as well. Textbooks for German schools offer a variety of information about London and New York, Stratford and San Francisco. Liverpool, however, is hardly ever mentioned. Non-fictional texts on this city could be included in a unit having *Educating Rita* as the central text for the purpose of providing the context that Willy Russell has in mind.

Liverpool is only a short distance from the seaside and from the impressive and beautiful scenery of the Lake District. Originally a natural harbour, a 'pool', the port of Liverpool was deepened and converted into a wet dock at the beginning of the 18th century and rebuilt and modernised after World War II. As it is a port, Liverpool is a very cosmopolitan city. There are a good number of Poles, Danes, Greeks, Ukrainians and West Indians in the city. Liverpool has the largest Roman Catholic diocese in Britain as a result of the fact that during the terrible potato famine in the 19th century many people left what is now the Republic of Ireland and settled in Liverpool.

Young people in Germany mostly associate Liverpool with the two football clubs Everton and Liverpool FC. Anfield Road, the grounds of Liverpool FC, rings a bell with many soccer fans as an awe-inspiring spot on the map of European Cup games. Football is almost a religion in Liverpool and according to the latest statistics, over 100,000 people in Liverpool either play or watch football regularly. Needless to say, the most famous Liverpudlians in the world are the Beatles. In a brochure published for the City of Liverpool Public Relations Office, Sarah Allen furnishes the reader with some interesting details on John, Paul, George and Ringo.

* Cf Interview (16 October 1996), Students' Book, pp. 110–111.

Sarah Allen, My Liverpool Home

The most famous Liverpudlians in the world must be the Beatles. John, Paul, George and Ringo started their incredible career performing at the now legendary Cavern Club, since pulled down to make way for the underground railway. During the 1960's they became cult figures. Their hair, their clothes, and even their Liverpool accents were copied everywhere. Because of the Beatles' success, lots of other groups sprang up in Liverpool, and a few became well known. Although the Beatles have now split up, and live and work in places as far apart as Los Angeles and the Mull of Kintyre, the group is commemorated in Liverpool by a plaque by Arthur Dooley on the wall opposite the site of the Cavern. This shows a mother figure, representing Liverpool, holding three cherubs, John, George and Ringo. Paul has wings *(Wings)* and is flying off on his own.

The Beatles were the main influence on pop music throughout the 1960's, the first non-Americans to achieve this since the turn of the century. The early music of Lennon and McCartney was simple and compulsive, such as *She Loves You* and *I Wanna Hold Your Hand*, but over the years their songs became more sophisticated, and in the late sixties and early seventies they were strongly influenced by music from India. The final split of the Beatles was partly because they were moving in different directions musically.

The shocked world reaction when John Lennon was shot dead in New York on 9th December 1980 showed how much people thought of him. Reaction was especially strong in Liverpool, his home town, where mourning fans gathered in Mathew Street, the site of the Cavern Club. As a tribute to Lennon the idealist, the seeker after peace and love, a Festival of Peace was held in Liverpool Anglican Cathedral on 29th March 1981. The Festival was in the form of a religious service, using the words and music of John Lennon, including some Lennon/McCartney songs, with prayers, hymns and songs on the theme of peace.

(Liverpool: Dinosaur Publications ^{2}1981, p. 28)

In the sixties, two famous Liverpudlian poets emerged from the Liverpool scene, Adrian Henri (born in 1932) and Roger McGough (born in 1937). Adrian Henri started in the music business and formed a band called *Liverpool Scene*. Later he moved on to writing poetry. Similarly, Roger McGough founded a pop group *(The Scaffold)*. *Lily the Pink* and *Thank you very much* were their most famous hits. When the group split up in 1975, Roger McGough, like Adrian Henri, began writing poetry. Henri's and McGough's poems are often very funny. They are written in ordinary language and help towards an understanding of what Liverpool poets write about. Editions of these poems are easily accessible, e.g.:

- Adrian Henri/Roger McGough/Brian Patten: *Penguin Modern Poets 10. The Mersey Sound.* Harmondsworth: Penguin 1967.
- Adrian Henri: *From the Loveless Motel. Poems 1976–1979.* London: Cape Paperbacks 1980.
- Roger McGough: *In the Classroom.* London: Cape Paperbacks 1979.
- Roger McGough: *Holiday on Death Row.* London: Cape Paperbacks 1981.

The following text can serve the purpose of introducing German students to Liverpool.

Liverpool

By some mysterious body chemistry most Liverpool children are born with the firm belief that their city is the centre of the universe. Give the earth a good nudge and its axis would undoubtedly protrude not at either of the poles but at the Pier Head. So it is a painful moment when they are first told that it did not even rate a mention in the Domesday Book. Fortunately, the pain is alleviated to some extent later when they learn that King John who signed *Magna Carta* in 1215 had signed another *carta* putting Liverpool on the map eight years earlier.

On the 28th August, 1207, to be precise, the king made Liverpool a borough and a port.

The king was looking for somewhere on the north-west coast where he could mount a plundering expedition to Ireland and *Liverpul* seemed to be just the place. It was no more than an obscure little fishing settlement but it had a pool which would serve to accommodate his ships. But first he had to develop it into more of a town so he issued his charter offering free land to all who would settle there. "... Wherefore we command that ye come thither unmolested and under our protection to receive and dwell in our burgage-holdings."

Although that was nearly eight hundred years ago Liverpool is really a comparatively modern city built over the last two hundred years and in a constant state of change ever since – especially during the last twenty-five years. And, in all truth, there really is nowhere on earth quite like it.

Most outsiders who come here for the first time and stay awhile, take in the general scene and savour the unique atmosphere admit this. Invariably it is nothing like what they expected. They know the legends, they have heard the songs, laughed at the comedians, and read the writers, but on stepping out of Lime Street Station for the first time they sense that, somehow, it is "you know – different".

For a start, the opening scene is not what they usually expect. Straight opposite is the St. John Centre, a modern complex of shops, a four-star hotel and restaurants, topped by St. John's Beacon, a tower thrusting four hundred and fifty feet towards the sun with a revolving restaurant just below the top, while over to the right, in absolute contrast, is St. George's Hall, one of the most magnificent (and largest) neo-Classical buildings in the whole of Europe. It took sixteen years to build and is as imposing inside as it is outside. Ever since the final stone was laid in 1854 celebrated writers and architects have used up all the adjectives of acclaim in describing it.

But this is really Liverpool's back door. To enter properly you should arrive by water. This is less likely to happen now than before the war when Liverpool was home port for the transatlantic liners and many cruise ships. Now you would have to be a seafarer, a visitor from Ireland or the Isle of Man, arrive from Birkenhead or Wallasey by ferry or be a passenger on an Aznar Line cruise.

For that matter, even if you have arrived by train at Lime Street it is worth taking the underground (that's usually another surprise) to Hamilton Square Station in Birkenhead. From there take a two-minute walk down to Woodside Landing Stage and take the boat across the Mersey. In this way you will be able to see one of the world's most impressive waterfronts – though it may well be familiar to you from watching television: it has been featured often enough.

(From: *This is Liverpool.* Published and issued by the City of Liverpool Public Relations Office.)

Topic 6

Educating Rita in German

Educating Rita has been produced in around thirty countries so far, including France, Spain, Holland, Austria, Turkey, Mexico, Denmark, and Germany. A German translation of the stage play was done by Angela Kingsford-Röhl (Litag-Theaterverlag, Bremen).

One of the main problems in translating the play arises from the fact that Rita speaks a language that is partly Scouse, partly also colloquial, or even slangy English. How is one to render this variety of English into German? Immediately one is inclined to think of the regional varieties of German spoken in Berlin or in Hessen or in the Ruhr district. But can they really be considered equivalents to Rita's language, which is not just a regional variety, not merely dialect? There are also the characteristics of the Open University, in fact of English university life in general, that do not have exact parallels in the German educational system.

The title of the play is, by no means, easy to translate. In Germany Russell's play (the stage play) is known under the title of *Bildung für Rita*. But is this an accurate rendering of the original English title? The word 'educate' has several connotations in English: 'to give intellectual and moral training to' (= bilden), 'to bring up young persons' (= aufziehen; erziehen), 'to provide schooling' (= ausbilden), 'to train a person' (= trainieren; drillen). From a grammatical point of view, the word 'educating' in *Educating Rita* can be a gerund (cf. 'reading books') or a present participle (cf. 'singing birds'). Hence the title is ambiguous. It can mean that Rita is being educated, it can also mean that Rita is educating someone else (cf. the ambiguity in 'visiting aunts can be tiresome', or 'flying planes can be dangerous'). This ambiguity in 'educating' is unfolded in the two acts of the play.

The film version of the play bears the German title *Rita will es endlich wissen*. This rendering has also two connotations, one being that Rita wants to know *it* (i.e. acquire a knowledge of English literature), the other that she is determined to put her plans into practice.

When translating scenes from *Educating Rita* the students must see to it that the connotations, the socio-cultural implications and metaphorical extensions of words and phrases are preserved in the German text.

For Classroom Work

For schools in those 'Bundesländer' in which "Translation" is part and parcel of the 'Schriftliche Abiturprüfung' the following two texts can help to practise translating from English into German.

A.

He'd stopped the cab. We still had another couple of miles to go before we got to the station. But we were stopped. And he was turned around, looking at me through the grill, his face wondering and intent, eyes wide and unblinking as he awaited the answer upon which, it seemed, his very life depended.

Why hadn't I lied? When we'd exhausted our views on weather and government (both of which we agreed were growing more appalling by the minute), when we'd grown tired of laughing at the daftness of princes and princesses, grown bored with bemoaning the increasing craziness of Christmas, when after lapsing into silence for a minute or two, he'd glanced at me in the rearview mirror and asked, 'So what is it that you do for a living?', why hadn't I lied and told him I was a teacher or a hairdresser or a warehouseman? Having, in the past, done all these jobs I could convincingly have kept up some sort of conversation if curiosity and politeness had required it. But I hadn't lied. I'd confessed.

'I write,' I whispered, 'write plays,' I reluctantly mumbled, turning and gazing out of the window, hoping that perhaps he hadn't quite heard me, wondering to myself about those times when I'd feverishly dreamed of the day when I could proudly, triumphantly, declare that what I was was a writer!

Willy Russell, *Plays: 1,* London: Methuen Drama, 1996.

B.

Frank sits in the swivel chair, facing her

Y' know at first I was dead scared. I didn't know anyone. I was gonna come home. But the first afternoon I was standin' in this library, y' know lookin' at the books, pretendin' I was dead clever. Anyway, this tutor come up to me, he looked at the book in me hand an' he said, 'Ah, are you fond of Ferlinghetti?' It was right on the tip of me tongue to say, 'Only when it's served with Parmesan cheese', but, Frank, I didn't. I held it back an' I heard meself sayin', 'Actually, I'm not too familiar with the American poets'. Frank, you woulda been dead proud of me. He started talkin' to me about the American poets – we sat around for ages – an' he wasn't even one of my official tutors, y' know. We had to go to this big hall for a lecture, there must have been two thousand of us in there. After he'd finished his lecture this professor asked if anyone had a question, an', Frank, I stood up! *(She stands)* Honest to God, I stood up, an' everyone's lookin' at me. I don't know what possessed me, I was gonna sit down again, but two thousand people had seen me stand up, so I did it, I asked him the question.

There is a pause and Frank waits.

(Willy Russell, *Educating Rita,* Act II, Scene 1, Students' Book, pp. 54-62)

4. Suggestions for Classroom Work

The following suggestions for dealing with *Educating Rita* in the foreign language classroom have all been tried and tested in an English 'Leistungskurs'. They do not form a complete teaching unit on the play but are to be thought of as ideas that can be worked into individually prepared lessons. Possible answers to the tasks or questions are given in boxes and incorporate suggestions made by students.

Pre-reading: Consulting the experts

As the title suggests, *Educating Rita* deals with an aspect of life every 'Oberstufen' student is an expert on – education. After at least six years of grammar school, virtually every student will hold firm views on the contents and quality of their own education. This expert knowledge can easily be tapped by assigning a number of pre-reading questions.

For example:

- Why did you choose grammar school?
- What do you expect to get out of your grammar school education?
- Has school so far lived up to your expectations? Why? Why not?

The evaluation of these questions will prepare the students for one of the play's central themes. More importantly, by making them reflect on the value and progress of their own experiences at school, they will be sensitized to Rita's quest for knowledge and thus be able to appreciate how her attitude to and expectations of education compare with their own. (Cf Section F in the Interview 16 October 1996)

Getting started: Assessing the opening scene of the play

Willy Russell says in an interview with Albert-Reiner Glaap that in a draft version of the play Frank was "an absolute vapid, colourless, almost off-stage cipher, a totally colourless man." When told by his agent

Peggy Ramsey that this sort of Frank was "totally useless", Russell realized that he had to write the play again and conceive Frank: "Instinctively I knew that if I was going to get Frank right, the play had to start with him." (Cf Students' Book, Interview 16 October 1996, p. 110)

This passage from the interview is as good a starting point as any to launch into an analysis of the play.

Step 1: Collecting criteria for an effective opening of a play

Pre-reading task: Work in groups of three or four. Consider what makes for a good, effective opening of a play and write a list of criteria.

Possible criteria:

The opening should

- offer a dramatic, punchy start to the play.
- arouse the audience's interest and curiosity.
- introduce the main characters and setting.
- plant the seeds of key themes early on.

Step 2: Assessing the quality of the opening of the play

Task: Read pp. 7-9
To what extent does the opening of *Educating Rita* meet the criteria you specified?

Possible answers:

Opening not dramatic but nevertheless effective because

- audience is thrown into the scene; no lengthy introduction.
- focus is on Frank – his job, his personal background, his drink problem.
- relevant background information is planted about on-stage and off-stage characters, e.g. Frank's relationship with a person he calls "darling", his reluctance to teach the O.U. course, his ambivalent attitude to the O.U. woman who is just about to arrive.
- the audience's curiosity is piqued. They want to know more about Frank and how his relationship with the people he refers to develops.

Step 3: Writing dialogue

Educating Rita is a product of revisions and clever craftsmanship. One aspect of craftsmanship to focus on is the way a playwright throws light on off-stage characters either through what the on-stage characters say about them, or by means of 'missing' dialogue in which only the on-stage character is heard, leaving the audience to guess at what the other person is saying. An example of this is Frank's telephone conversation with the person he refers to as 'darling'.

Task: Work with a partner. Rewrite the phone call, adding the lines you think the other person is saying.
Two or three pairs can be asked to present their versions to the class, and these versions can be compared. The class discusses whether or not the opening of the play would benefit from the inclusion of the added lines.

Possible comments:

- The lines spoken by the person at the other end are unnecessary because the audience can work out very easily for themselves what the unheard part of the dialogue might be.
- The audience's interest is aroused as to who this person called 'darling' is and why Frank reacts to her the way he does.

Frank and Rita at the beginning of Scenes 1 and 2

Reading the script of a play has one important advantage over watching its performance on stage: the reader has the opportunity to pause whenever he or she likes, read the lines again and reflect on what has happened and how the play might develop. The 'blackout' at the end of Scene 1 is an obvious place for such a pause. Scene 1 ends on a cliffhanger when Frank tells Rita in unambiguous terms that she is "not coming here next week." A question likely to be foremost on the reader's mind will be whether or not Rita will come back to Frank's tutorial and, if she does, how the meetings with him might continue.

Step 1: Speculating about how the play will continue

Task: Work in twos or threes. Based on what you know about Frank and Rita from Scene 1, jot down in your journals how you think the play might continue in Scene 2. What possible developments do you expect? Why?

Step 2: Comparing the openings of two scenes

The development that Frank and Rita undergo during the course of the two acts adds momentum and suspense to the play. It can best be plotted by a comparison of scenes. The openings of Act I, Scenes 1 and 2 lend themselves to such a task. (Later in the play, a comparison of Act I, Scene 1 with Act II, Scene 1 helps to show how far Rita has progressed in her academic aspirations.)

Tasks: Read Scene 2, pp. 21-29
In groups of twos or threes compare the openings of Scenes 1 and 2. What are the similarities and differences?
Have Frank and Rita undergone any changes since the beginning of the play?

Evaluation:

	Scene 1	**Scene 2**
Setting:	• Frank's office	• Frank's office
Characters:	• Frank and Rita	• Frank and Rita
Character development:	**Frank** • Reservations about teaching O.U. from the very start; does not want Rita to come again. • Slightly confused, almost speechless after Rita forced her way through the jammed door.	**Frank** • Looks forward to Rita's arrival; glances at his watch repeatedly. • His manner is more inviting; offers Rita his chair.
	Rita • Determined and enthusiastic; literally forces her way through the jammed door. • Practical, confident;	**Rita** • Determined and practical; comes in after oiling the door. • Confident, outspoken; tells Frank that she never expected him

	advises Frank to do something about the jammed door.	to get around to oiling the door.

Step 3: Interpreting symbolic meanings

The fact that the setting and the characters are identical focuses the reader's attention on the dialogue itself and the behaviour of the two characters. It also draws the reader's interest to words that are used symbolically and thereby illuminate aspects of the characters. This aspect will be at the centre of the next assignment.

Task: Look at words with symbolic meanings at the beginning of Scenes 1 and 2 and speculate as to what they suggest about Frank and Rita.

Possible comments/conclusions:

Symbol	What it suggests about Frank	What it suggests about Rita
The jammed door	• Shows that Frank is cut off from the world outside, perhaps even trapped. • Underlines that Frank is in danger of being isolated in his 'ivory tower'.	• Symbolic of how Rita sees the cloistered world of the university. • Suggests that Frank's world is off-limits to people like Rita.
The can of oil	• Indicates that Frank is an impractical academic.	• Highlights Rita's pragmatic nature. • Depicts Rita as a potential 'liberator' who saves Frank from getting stuck inside. • Oiling the door shows that Rita is serious about ensuring her access to a world that means so much to her.

Frank's and Rita's understanding of 'culture'

The gulf that separates Rita's world from the one Frank lives in is brought into focus when the dialogue between them turns to the word 'culture'. While Rita maintains that she has "got no culture", Frank retorts "Of course you have." Why is there this disagreement? Who is right and who is wrong? Does Rita's learned professor know more about her working-class background than she herself? Or does the confusion arise simply because teacher and student have different definitions in mind when they think of 'culture'? An analysis of Frank and Rita's respective interpretations of the word 'culture' in Act I, Scene 4 helps explain why the two characters have a serious argument in Scene 7.

Step 1: Defining the word 'culture'

Tasks: (Optional)

1. Brainstorming: What do you associate with the word 'culture'?
   Jot down possible definitions.
2. Study the definitions of the word 'culture' in your dictionary.
   Compare them with the ideas you have written down.

Step 2: Applying the dictionary definitions to Frank's and Rita's conceptions of culture

Tasks:

1. Analyse Act I, Scene 4, pp. 35 (10)-36 (32) and give a presentation of the different views expressed by Frank and Rita.
2. Look at the dictionary definitions of the word 'culture' again and work out which of them fits their respective conceptions of culture.

Evaluation:

Culture

Rita	**Frank**
"We've got no culture." (35) • Thinks of culture in terms of "a refined understanding and appreciation of art, literature etc."* • Sees herself as having no culture since she is working-class and uneducated. • Is under the impression that education is the key to acquiring culture.	"Of course you have." (35) • Thinks of culture in terms of the "customs of a particular group, e.g. working-class culture."* "There's nothing wrong with that, if they're content with it." (35) • Has an idealized view of the working-class culture.

Step 3:

Tasks:
1. Prepare a dramatized reading of Scene 7, pp. 48 (28)-50 (28) at home and present it in class.
2. Explain whether Rita's failure to attend Frank's dinner party can be explained in terms of the two different conceptions of 'culture' we analyzed in Scene 4.

* Cf *Oxford Advanced Learner's Dictionary of Current English.*

Evaluation:

Rita's dilemma

Frank	**Rita**
1. Has a sincere personal interest in Rita being at his party: • "They would have seen someone who's funny, delightful, charming ..." • "I just wanted you to be yourself." 3. Rejects Rita's assumption as wrong and blows up: • "If you believe that that's why you were invited [...] you can get out, now."	2. Assumes that Frank wants to show her off as a representative of her working-class culture: • "Bring her in because she's good for a laugh." • "I don't wanna be funny." • "I didn't come to your house to play the court jester." 4. An identity crisis is triggered off in Rita : • "I can't talk to the people I live with anymore. An' I can't talk to the likes of them on Saturday ... I'm a half-caste."

Conclusion: By the end of Act I Rita finds herself suspended in a no man's land between two classes. She is alienated from her own working-class culture which she despises. At the same time she feels out of place amongst people whose education has given them the sort of culture she is aspiring to, i.e. a refined understanding of art and literature.

The theme of self-realization

Rita's development, her quest for knowledge, is a young woman's personal attempt at realizing her intellectual potential. This journey of self-discovery takes her from the familiar surroundings of her working-class environment into the unknown territory of an Open University education. Her quest for knowledge does not take place in a vacuum but is subject to the push and pull of people at home, at work, at the Open University, etc. When one contrasts Rita's values with those held by the people around her, the extent of her achievement is all the more remarkable.

Tasks: 1. Some characters in the stage version of *Educating Rita* are only "off-stage" characters, i.e. they are only referred to in the dialogue between Rita and Frank. Make a list of these characters.
2. Say which of these characters should make an appearance in the screen version of the play, and explain why.
3. Make a list of the values associated with or introduced by the off-stage characters and compare them with those held by Rita and Frank.

Evaluation:

Characters	**Idea of self-realization**
On-stage	
• Rita	• changing oneself from the inside (17); discovering oneself (18); being able to write and understand literary criticism (71); knowing "what clothes to wear, what wine to buy, what plays to see, what papers and books to read" (74); having choice by being educated (77)
• Frank	• taking Rita by her hand and running out of his study forever (29); going to the pub and getting drunk to make himself believe that "under all the talk one is actually saying something" (41)
Off-stage	
• Denny	• saving money in order to move to a more expensive house in a fashionable suburb (18-19); having a good time at the pub where one can choose from amongst eight different kinds of lager (40); family life and children (51)
• Rita's customers	• changing oneself by getting a new hairstyle (17)

• Rita's mates on the estate	• not being different from one's mates (23); "music an' clothes an' lookin' for a feller" (23)
• Trish	• "being dead classy" (57); "a flat that is dead unpretentious, just books an' plants everywhere" (57) "eatin' wholefoods an' health foods" (76)

Frank's attitude to Rita as reflected in his criticisms of her literary work

The play chronicles Rita's development from an uneducated hairdresser to a sophisticated O.U. graduate. The obstacles she has to overcome are many. While at first she is ignorant of the difference between pulp and serious fiction, even confusing Foster the brewery with Forster the novelist, or Yates the wine lodge with Yeats the poet, she gradually picks up the 'tricks of the trade', learns to write literary criticism and in the end passes her finals "with distinction".

It is from Rita's academic development and the response it draws from Frank that the play derives its tension. A systematic analysis of Frank's criticisms of Rita's literary work shows, for instance, that throughout Act I her academic progress is unsatisfactory. It is not until she returns from summer school at the beginning of Act II that her essays begin to show signs of promise, forcing Frank to admit grudgingly that they "would not look out of place" with the ones written by the 'real' university students. Frank seems to prefer the freshness and frankness of her 'unacademic' work. The reader senses that Frank is becoming increasingly cynical about the value of literary criticism just as Rita is beginning to come to terms with it. Also, Rita's growing confidence and her mastery of literary criticism symbolize her independence from Frank, which makes him resentful. The relationship between them turns sour, climaxing in their ferocious argument in Act II, Scene 5.

Step 1: An analysis of Frank's criticisms of Rita's academic progress

Task: 1. Study Frank's advice on how to approach English literature as shown in his criticisms of Rita's essays and comments, and complete the worksheet.

Evaluations: Cf worksheets on the following two pages

Step 2: Frank's changing attitude to Rita during Acts I and II

Tasks/Questions:

1. Comment on Frank's criticism. Does anything strike you as interesting or confusing?
2. Why does Frank insist on an approach to literature in Act II that he would have despised in Act I?
3. What do Frank's comments reveal about himself?

Step 3: *Educating Rita:* A Love Story?

In the preface to the play Russell says that "when making *Educating Rita* I tried very hard to write a love story." (p. 6)

Task: Go over the text and find evidence that proves or refutes the author's statement.

Evaluations: Cf chapter 2.2, A Love Story?, pp. 28–30.

Gunther Volk

Frank's attitude to Rita as reflected in his criticisms (1-7) of her academic progress

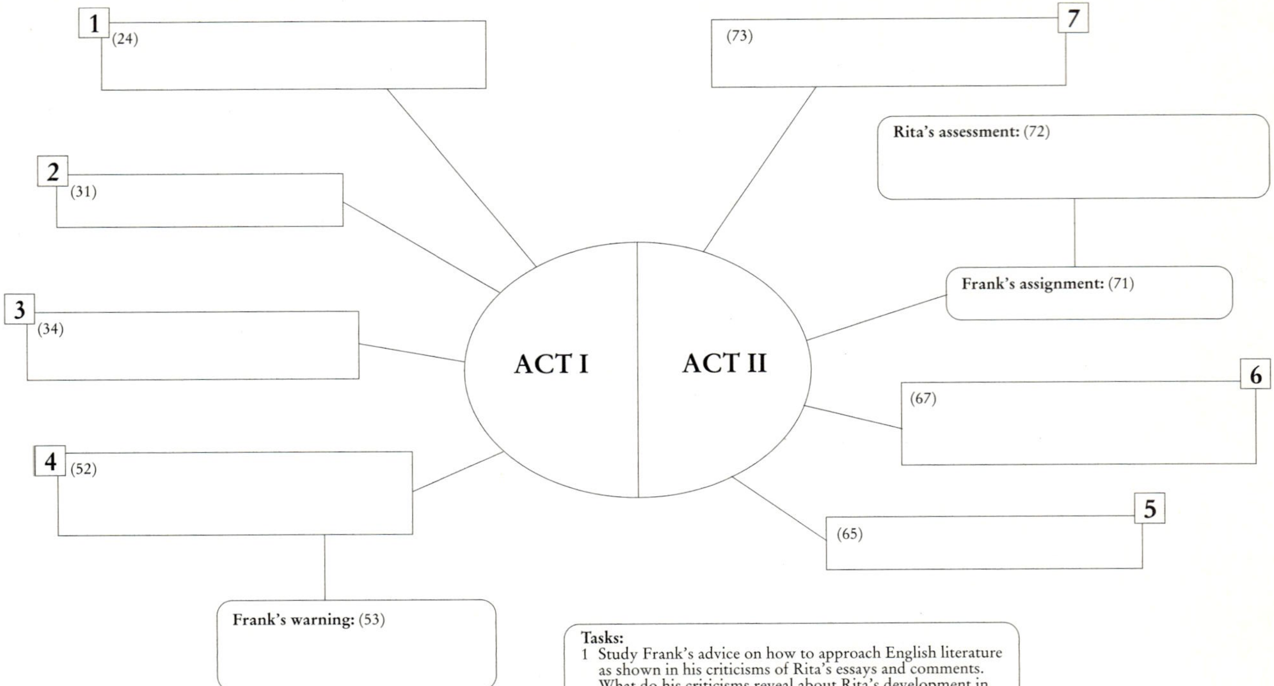

Tasks:
1 Study Frank's advice on how to approach English literature as shown in his criticisms of Rita's essays and comments. What do his criticisms reveal about Rita's development in Acts I and II?
2 What do Frank's comments reveal about himself?

Gunther Volk (1997)

Frank's attitude to Rita as reflected in his criticisms (1-7) of her academic progress

ACT I

1 "It was an appreciation, a descriptive piece. What you have to learn is criticism … Criticism is purely objective … In criticism sentiment has no place." (24)

2 "You seem to be under the impression that all books are literature." (31)

3 An essay is more than just a sentence. It must contain considered argument(s) and "quotes from accepted authorities." (34)

4 "It's a totally honest, passionate account of your reaction to a play … But in terms of what you're asking me to teach you of passing exams … in those terms it's worthless." (52)

Frank's warning: "You are going to have to suppress, perhaps even abandon your uniqueness. I'm going to have to change you." (53)

ACT II

5 "Oh – it – erm – wouldn't look out of place with these. … Dead honest." (65)

6 "seem to assume that this poem is about sexuality. … It's up to the minute, quite acceptable, trendy stuff about Blake; but there's nothing of you in there." (67)

Assignment: "A critical assessment of a lesser known English poet. Me." (71)

Rita's assessment: "This is brilliant. They're witty. They're profound. Full of style. … You can see in it a direct line through to nineteenth century traditions of – of like wit an' classical allusion." (72)

7 "You recognize the hallmark of literature now, don't you? Why don't you just go away. I don't think I can bear it any longer." (73)

Questions for analysis:

1 What do the criticisms reveal about Rita's development?
2 Why does Frank insist on an approach to literature in Act II that he would have despised in Act I ?
3 What do Frank's comments reveal about himself?

Gunther Volk (1997)

Educating Rita ...
... this, that and the other

Encouraging various activities

Describe the cover picture of the Students' Book and relate it to the beginning (p. 20) and the end (p. 78) of the play.

- "you're the first breath of air that's been in this room" (p. 18)
- "The room needs airing" (p. 58)

Comment.

Explain the title of Russell's play and suggest an adequate German title.

Point out and explain details of the cartoon in the Students' Book.

Which questions about *Educating Rita* would you ask the playwright?

"The Sick Rose" (p. 60)
Write a parody on the poem.

Being a ... in a Theatre.

... Director
What kind of stage would you choose for *Educating Rita*? (Theatre-in-the Round? Proscenium arch? or ...?)

... Costume Designer
What sort of dress should Rita wear? Should it change in the course of the play?

... Press Officer
Design a poster to advertise a production of *Educating Rita*.

... Translator
What kind of language register/ dialect/sociolect should a German actress speak?

... Stage (Set) Designer
What furnishings would you suggest for the tutorial room?

... Film Critic
Write a brief review of the film *Educating Rita*.

(1.) The Lights come up on Frank who is sitting in the armchair listening to the radio. Rita enters, goes straight to the desk and slings her bag on the back of her chair. (Act I, Scene 7)

(2.) The Lights come up on Rita who is sitting in the armchair by the window, reading a heavy tome. There is the sound of muffled oaths from behind the door. Frank enters carrying his briefcase. He is very drunk. (Act II, Scene 3)

Compare these introductory stage directions with regard to the relationship between Rita and Frank.

5. Suggestions for Tests

The first of the following tests was given to students in an English Leistungskurs 12/2 (Theodor-Heuss-Schule, Ratingen). I would like to thank their teacher, Ingrid Hartmann-Scheer for kindly making the material available. The second test was developed and selected for the 'Schriftliches Abitur (Grundkurs)'. Thanks are due to Karin Feilen and Ingrid Hartmann-Scheer. The third test was given as an oral exam by Gunther Volk (Gymnasium am Romäusring, Villingen-Schwenningen).

First Test

English: Leistungskurs, 12/2

After reading and discussing Willy Russell's *Educating Rita* in class the students were asked to study an excerpt from E.M. Forster's *Two Cheers for Democracy* and answer the four questions listed below. The paper reprinted on the following pages was written by Dorothea Weiland (Theodor-Heuss-Schule). No alterations whatsoever have been undertaken for publication purposes. This applies both to content and language.

E.M. Forster, The Raison D'Être Of Criticism In The Arts

Most of us will agree that previous training is desirable before we approach the arts. We mistrust untrained appreciation, believing that it often defeats its own ends. Appreciation ought to be enough. But unless we learn by example and by failure and by comparison, appreciation will not bite. We shall tend to slip about on the surface of masterpieces, exclaiming with joy, but never penetrating. "Oh, I do like Bach," cries one appreciator, and the other cries, "Do you? I don't. I like Chopin." Exit in opposite directions chanting Bach and Chopin respectively, and hearing less the composers than their own voices. They resemble investors who proclaim the soundness of their financial assets. The Bach shares must not fall, the Chopin not fall farther, or one would have been proved a fool on the aesthetic stock exchange. The objection to untrained appreciation is not its naïveté but its tendency to lead to the appreciation of no one but oneself. Against such fatuity the critical spirit is a valuable corrective.

Except at the actual moment of contact – and I shall have much to say on the subject of that difficult moment – it is desirable to know why we like a work, and to be able to defend our preferences by argument. Our judgement has been strengthened and if all goes well the contacts will be intensified and increased and become more valuable.

I add the proviso 'if all goes well' because success lies on the knees of an unknown God. There is always the contrary danger; the danger that training may sterilize the sensitiveness that is being trained; that education may lead to knowledge instead of wisdom, and criticism to nothing but criticism; that spontaneous enjoyment, like the Progress of Poesy in Matthew Arnold's poem, may be checked because too much care has been taken to direct it into the right channel. Still it is a risk to be faced, and if no care had been taken the stream might have vanished even sooner. We hope criticism will help. We have faith in it as a respectable human activity, as an item in the larger heritage which differentiates us from the beasts.

(In: *Two Cheers for Democracy.* Harmondsworth: Penguin 1974, pp. 115–116.)

Annotations:
previous (l. I) – former; **exit** (l. 8) – here: they go away; **investor** (l. 9) – someone who puts money in e.g. business; **asset** (l. 10) – Vermögen, Werte; **share** (l. 11) – Aktie, Wertpapier; **stock exchange** (l. 12) – Börse; **fatuity** (l. 14) – foolishness; **proviso** (l. 21) – Einschränkung; **to vanish** (l. 28) – to disappear.

Tasks:

1. What are, according to Forster, the advantages and disadvantages of untrained appreciation and criticism?
2. The author himself is a writer and literary critic. Point out two stylistic features that reflect these two sides.
3. Compare E.M. Forster's opinion about the untrained appreciation of art and the function of criticism with Rita's and Frank's approach to literature at the beginning of Russell's play.
4. Do you think that "previous training is desirable before we approach the arts" (ll. 1–2)? Give reasons for your answer.

The following paper was written by Dorothea Weiland (Theodor-Heuss-Schule, Ratingen) on the above mentioned tasks. No alterations whatsoever have been undertaken for publication purposes. This applies to both content and language.

1. The text deals with people's approach to the arts. On the one hand, there is, as E. M. Forster calls it, the "untrained appreciation", on the

other hand there is criticism. Both have their advantages and disadvantages. Somebody who thinks he can judge a piece of art without being able to give reasons, without any knowledge about the background of it will not come as near to it as somebody who has been trained. Often he will stay on the surface, he will praise or condemn it out of a moment's emotion. Also he tends to be strongly influenced by fashion. Forster compares that to a stock exchange where you learn the different values of Bach, Chopin and other composers and artists. But untrained appreciation is not always wrong. A lot of people have a natural sensitiveness and can distinguish between good and bad works. Also there is more spontaneity in it if you enjoy something just because you like it and not because someone told you that it is extraordinary and one must like it. Enjoyment like that resulting from one's spontaneous approach sometimes doesn't last very long. Criticism is helpful here because it makes people discover other sides of a piece of art and allows them to reach depths they never thought of before. Training may teach you to see or hear with other people's eyes or ears, you learn what they think about it. And if somebody asks you why you prefer Bach to Chopin you will be able to say more than "Oh, I just love that music." In doing this, your own behaviour will maybe become clearer to you. The other side of the coin is that criticism can destroy your sensitiveness and, as Forster says, "lead to knowledge instead of wisdom". You may lose your fun and you would now be influenced not by fashion but by established critique. But for the author these disadvantages don't weigh that much. Criticism and critical education if they are carefully dealt with build up sensitivity rather than destroy it.

2. E. M. Forster, the author of this text, is not only a literary critic but a writer himself. These two traits (of his character) are both expressed in this text. The literary critic develops his arguments in a logical way. He often uses contrasts to make clear what he means. Comparing these pairs of contradictory statements or opinions he gradually works out his own ideas. (For example in lines 21–27: as he speaks about the danger lying in criticism and education to criticism there is at first the contrast to the second part, then three pairs of contradictions follow: "that training may sterilize the sensitiveness that is being trained; that education may lead to knowledge instead of wisdom, and criticism to nothing but criticism" and finally he brings a counter-argument to that thesis again.) As a writer Forster uses several images to depict his theory. People who just appreciate a masterpiece "slip about on the surface". In the way he describes the scene between the Bach and the Chopin admirer one could

nearly see it on stage, he even seems to give stage directions ("exit in opposite directions chanting Bach and Chopin respectively"). He compares the public opinion about arts and artists with a stock exchange and the different personal ideas with shares. The enjoyment of a piece of art is shown as a stream which is at first wild and uncontrolled but then may vanish quickly spending its forces use- and senselessly if it is not directed into the right channel. These images used as a stylistic feature together with the critic's contrasts make the text somewhat like a speech. Forster unites those two sides – the one of the writer and the one of the literary critic – without any difficulties to a harmonic result.

3. The two methods of approaching pieces of art – untrained appreciation and criticism – are somewhat personified by Rita and Frank in Russell's play "Educating Rita". At the beginning of the play Rita does exactly the things Forster describes. She likes something without being able to explain why; she dislikes, for example, one of Forster's works "Howard's End" for ridiculous reasons because she doesn't know what the author wants to say. She also shows no interest in other people's opinions about it; she couldn't care less. Frank calls her way of dealing with literature "partisan interpretation". He has to teach her literary criticism because this is the theme of the Open University course she has enrolled for. His opinions about a piece of literature are characterized – at least at the beginning of the play – by objectivity. They are based on his knowledge about the historical, social and personal background of the author and on established literary critique. He knows why he likes or dislikes something – sometimes this question even has no significance for him because his personal opinions are not important at all. What other famous critics say has more weight. "Educating Rita" doesn't mention all the disadvantages of either Rita's or Frank's dealing with literature. Rita wants real education, she wants to be educated and not just to seem so. She hasn't any information about the (to say it in Forster's words) "aesthetic stock exchange". Frank hasn't lost his sensitiveness, no, it has been well trained. He is still open for new ways.

4. In my opinion education is quite important as a basis for people's approach to a piece of art. All opinions and judgements we form in our mind – whether we tell someone or not – result from our place in society and our personal history of life. Education is a significant factor. Spontaneous approach is nice and you may well enjoy, for example, a painting by Picasso but you will not see it as intensively as someone who knows something about the historical background, about the style and maybe what Picasso wanted to say. He doesn't just like or dislike it but has an

opinion founded on facts. I also see the danger of overeducating someone, of fixing his thoughts in a way that they are not thoughts of his own any more. Education – especially in the area of arts – should be handled very carefully to avoid this destruction of personal ideas. It should show the way to those ideas of one's own because educating a person means more than just training him to distinguish between good and bad pieces of art. It gives the direction – but you must find your own path through the museum of arts, you are the one who decides what you think. This is something that criticism should never even touch.

Second Test

English: Grundkurs, Schriftliches Abitur

The following text is taken from Willy Russell's *Educating Rita* (pp. 22–24). The play was not studied in class. But non-fictional texts on "Education and the Educational System in England" were dealt with in a thematic unit in grade 12 (Theodor-Heuss-Schule, Ratingen).

Rita It looks the way I always imagined a public school to look, y' know a boardin' school. When I was a kid I always wanted to go to a boardin' school.

Frank God forbid it; why?

Rita *(going to her chair at the desk)* I always thought they sounded great, schools like that, y' know with a tuck-shop an' a matron an' prep. An' a pair of kids called Jones minor an' Jones major. I told me mother once. *(She opens her bag and takes out the copy of "Howards End", ring bound file, note-pad, ruler and pencil-case, placing them methodically on the desk in front of her)* She said I was off me cake.

Frank *(with an exaggerated look at her)* What in the name of God is being off one's cake?

Rita Soft. Y' know, mental.

Frank Aha. I must remember that. The next student to ask me if Isabel Archer was guilty of protestant masochism shall be told that one is obviously very off one's cake!

Rita Don't be soft. You can't say that.

Frank Whyever not?

Rita You can't. If you do it, it's slummin' it. Comin' from you it'd sound dead affected, wouldn't it?

Frank Dead affected?

Rita Yeh. You say that to your proper students they'll think you're off your – y' know …

Frank Cake, yes. Erm – Rita, why didn't you ever become what you call a proper student?

Rita What? After goin' to the school I went to?

Frank Was it bad?

Rita starts sharpening the pencils one by one into perfect spikes, leaving the shavings on the desk

Rita Nah, just normal, y' know; borin', ripped-up books, broken glass everywhere, knives an' fights. An' that was just in the staffroom. Nah, they tried their best I suppose, always tellin' us we stood more of a chance if we studied. But studyin' was just for the whimps, wasn't it? See, if I'd started takin' school seriously I would have had to become different from me mates, an' that's not allowed.

Frank By whom?

Rita By your mates, by your family, by everyone. So y' never admit that school could be anythin' other than useless.

Frank passes her the ashtray but she ignores it and continues sharpening the pencils on to the table

Like what you've got to be into is music an' clothes an' lookin' for a feller, y' know the real qualities of life. Not that I went along with it so reluctantly. I mean, there was always somethin' in me head, tappin' away, tellin' me I might have got it all wrong. But I'd just play another record or buy another dress an' stop worryin'. There's always somethin' to make you forget about it. So y' do, y' keep goin', tellin' yourself life's great. There's always another club to go to, a new feller to be chasin', a laugh an' a joke with the girls. Till, one day, y' own up to yourself an' y' say, is this it? Is this the absolute maximum I can expect from this livin' lark? An' that's the big moment that one, that's the point when y' have to decide whether it's gonna be another change of dress or a change in yourself. An' it's really temptin' to go out an' get another dress y' know, it is. Cos it's easy, it doesn't cost anythin', it doesn't upset anyone around y'. Like cos they don't want y' to change.

This scene consists of 540 words.

Annotations: **Jones major** (7) – the older boy called Jones; **Jones minor** (7) – the younger boy called Jones; **Howards End** (8) – novel by E.M. Forster (1910); **Isabel Archer** (14)-heroine of Henry James' novel *The Portrait of a Lady;* **to slum it** (19) – to behave and live in a way below your social position; **whimps** (32) – weak, spineless characters

Tasks:

1. In how far is a boarding school as Rita imagines it different from the school she went to?
2. Point out why Rita did not become a proper student.
3. Explain the reasons that made Rita take a course in literature at the Open University.
4. Point out typical linguistic elements that characterize Rita as a member of the working-class. Give examples from the text.
5. What does Rita hope to find through education [school]? In what way do you think can education [school] help her to achieve her aim?

Third Test

English: Mündliches Abitur

Educating Rita

The RSC Warehouse is revealing an unhappy knack of eliciting bad plays from good young playwrights. Their latest production is a predictable two-hander by Willy Russell, one of the new Liverpool school. He needs encouragement on big stages, and a flop at the Warehouse like a hole in the head.

Even though plotting has never been Mr Russell's strong point, I think of his work as Alan Ayckbourn with a hairy chest and a hang-over. His mouthpiece this time is a 26-year-old frustrated housewife seeking escape through the Open University. Where the playwright is most sympathetic is in his passionate enunciation, through Rita, of education as a fundamental human right, at least in our comparatively developed society.

Rita's Svengali is an alcoholic red brick English lecturer who admires her instincts in preferring Harold Robbins to E.M. Forster but teaches her to write essays in the hollow academic style he despises himself for propagating. (...) Rita's solution to the problems of staging *Peer Gynt* – "do it on the radio" – could apply to the play itself. It has little dramatic invention or momentum and is not helped by a faceless characterisation of the lecturer by Mark Kingston.

(Michael Coveney, *Financial Times*, 17 June 1980.)

Annotations:
RSC (1) – Royal Shakespeare Company; **knack** – talent; **to elicit** – to draw out; **two-hander** (3) – play for two actors; **plotting** (6) – Konstruktion der Handlung; **enunciation** (10) – here: statement on; **Svengali** (13) – here: mentor; **to propagate** (16) – here: to spread more widely (verbreiten)

Tasks:

1. Summarize what Michael Coveney liked and did not like about *Educating Rita* at the performance he saw.
2. Describe how the theme of education is developed in the play.

6. Select Bibliography

Secondary Literature on *Educating Rita*

Debusscher, Gilbert: "Educating Rita or, an Open University Pygmalion." In: Gilbert Debusscher and van Noppen (eds.) *Communicating and Translating.* Bruxelles: 1985, 303–317.

Gill, John (ed.): *Willy Russell And His Plays.* Birkenhead, Wirral, Merseyside: Countyvise Limited 1992.

Glaap, Albert-Reiner: "'Educating Rita': Literatur für Jedermann. Zur Interpretation einer Komödie von Willy Russell." In: *Der fremdsprachliche Unterricht,* Heft 62, 1982, 108–121.

Glaap, Albert-Reiner: "Für einen 'offenen Kanon'. Zeitgenössische englische Dramen als Schullektüren, Identifikationsangebote und Gesprächsanlässe." In: Hunfeld, Hans (ed.), *Literaturwissenschaft – Literaturdidaktik – Literaturunterricht: Englisch. II. Eichstätter Kolloquium zum Fremdsprachenunterricht 1981.* Königstein/Ts.: Scriptor 1982, 178–190.

Ruge, Enno: "Literatur als Bildung? Willy Russells Drama 'Educating Rita' im Unterricht." In: *Fremdsprachenunterricht* 2/1997, 86–91.

References to literary works in *Educating Rita*

Blake, William: *Songs of Innocence & of Experience.* Oxford: Oxford University Press 1977.

Blake, William: *Lieder der Unschuld und der Erfahrung.* Hofmann, Werner (ed.), Frankfurt/M.: Insel 1975.

Brown, Rita Mae: *Rubyfruit Jungle.* London: Corgi Books 1978.

Eliot, Thomas Stearns: "The Love Song of J. Alfred Prufrock." In: *Collected Poems 1909–1962.* London: Faber 1974.

Forster, Edward Morgan: *Howards End.* Harmondsworth: Penguin 1946.

James, Henry: *The Portrait of a Lady.* Oxford: Oxford University Press 1989.

Lawrence, David Herbert: *Lady Chatterley's Lover.* Harmondsworth: Penguin 1978.

Lawrence, David Herbert: *Sons and Lovers.* Harmondsworth: Penguin 1981.

Maugham, William Somerset: *Of Human Bondage.* London: Pan Books 1975.

Robbins, Harold: *A Stone for Danny Fisher.* London: New English Library 1979.

Shakespeare, William: *Macbeth.* Harlow (Essex): Longman 1982.

Shakespeare's Macbeth. Kursmodell Englisch. Emunds, Karl (ed.): Schülerbuch, Video, Lehrerhandreichung. München: Langenscheidt-Longman 1983.

Wilde, Oscar: *The Importance of Being Earnest.* London: Eyre Methuen 1981.

Other references

Shaw, Bernard: *Pygmalion.* London: Penguin Books 1957.

Shaw Bernard: *Pygmalion.* Burnt Mill, Harlow: Longman 1991.

On Pygmalion

Kugler-Euerle, Gabriele: "Educating Eliza, Rita and Frank! Rezeptionsorientierte Vorschläge zur Behandlung von Bernard Shaws 'Pygmalion' and Willy Russells 'Educating Rita' im Englischunterricht der Sekundarstufe II." In: *Fremdsprachenunterricht* 2/1997, 91–98.

Otten, Kurt: "George Bernard Shaw: 'Pygmalion'." In: Horst Oppel (ed.), *Das moderne englische Drama*. Berlin: Erich Schmidt Verlag 1966.

Otten, Kurt/Rohmann, Gerd (eds.), *Bernard Shaw*. Darmstadt: Wissenschaftliche Buchgesellschaft 1978.

Fictional texts on education

Causley, Charles: "Timothy Winters." In: *Collected Poems 1951–1975*. London: Macmillan 1975.

Dickens, Charles: *Hard Times*. Harmondsworth: Penguin 1969.

Gray, Simon: *Quartermaine's Terms*. London: Eyre Methuen 1981.

Hines, Barry: *Kes*. Harmondsworth: Penguin 1982.

Hughes, Thomas: *Tom Brown's School Days*. New York: Airmont Publishing Company 1968.

Lass, Abraham H./Tasmann, Norma L. (eds.): *Going to School. An Anthology of Prose about Teachers and Students*. New York: Mentor Books 1980.

McMillan, Michael: *The School Leaver*. London: Black Ink Collective 1978.

Mitchell, Julian: *Another Country*. Ashover: Amber Lane Press 1982.

O'Malley, Mary: *Once a Catholic*. Ashover: Amber Lane Press 1978.

Orwell, George: "Boys' Weeklies." In: *Inside the Whale and Other Essays*. Harmondsworth: Penguin 1962, pp. 175–203.

Saunders, James: "The Pedagogue." In: *Neighbours and Other Plays*. London: Andre Deutsch 1968.

Spark, Muriel: *The Prime of Miss Jean Brodie*. Harmondsworth: Penguin 1977.

Stoppard, Tom: "Where Are They Now." In: *Artist Descending a Staircase & Where Are They Now*. London: Faber 1973.

Wesker, Arnold: "Roots." In: *The Wesker Trilogy*. Harmondsworth: Penguin 1977.

Whitehead, Ted: "The Punishment." In: Durband, Alan (ed.), *Prompt Three – Five Short Modern Plays*. London: Hutchinson 1976.

Whitman, Walt: "When I Heard the Learn'd Astronomer." In: Blodgett, Harold W./Bradley, Scully (eds.), *Leaves of Grass*. New York: University Press 1965.

Non-fictional texts on education

Der fremdsprachliche Unterrricht, Heft 70 (Schulsysteme – Informationen und Unterrichtsmaterialien), 1984.

Doyé, Peter: *The Language of Education*. Königstein/Ts.: Scriptor 1981.

Fiedler, Eckhard/Christie, David (eds.): *Going to School – Education in Britain*. Paderborn: Schöningh 1981.

Häußler, Karl J.: "Die Schulwelt im Umbruch: Der englische Schulroman der sechziger und siebziger Jahre." In: *anglistik & englischunterricht* 19, 1983, S. 139–160.

Hunfeld, Hans: "Individuelle Erfahrung und literarische Spiegelung: Englische und amerikanische 'school stories' von William Saroyan bis Donald Barthelme." In: Freese, Peter/Groene, Horst/Hermes, Liesel (eds.), *Die Short*

Story im Englischunterricht der Sekundarstufe II. Paderborn: Schöningh, 1979, S. 330–356.
Kuebart, Friedrich: *"Mitbestimmung im englischen Schulwesen. Probleme der 'Schuldemokratie' im Lichte des Taylor-Reports." In:* anglistik & englischunterricht 10, 1980, S. 171–190.
Rieger, Volker/Ulmer, Gerd: *Education – A Programmed Course on Educational Problems based on Authentic Texts.* Frankfurt/M.: Diesterweg 1976.

Books on contemporary British drama

Berney, K.A. (ed.): *Contemporary British Dramatists.* London: St. James Press 1994.
Elsom, John: *Post-war British Theatre.* London: Routledge & Kegan Paul 1976.
Elsom, John: *Post-war British Theatre Criticism.* London: Routledge & Kegan Paul 1981.
Hayman, Ronald: *Theatre and Anti-theatre. New Movements since Beckett.* London: Secker & Warburg 1979.
Innes, Christopher: *Modern British Drama 1890–1990.* Cambridge: Cambridge University Press 1992.
Itzin, Catherine: *Stages in the Revolution. Political Theatre in Britain since 1968.* London: Eyre Methuen 1980.
Kosok, Heinz (ed.): *Drama und Theater im England des 20. Jahrhunderts.* Düsseldorf: Bagel 1980.
Müller, K.P. (ed.): *Englisches Theater der Gegenwart. Geschichte(n) und Strukturen.* Tübingen: Gunter Narr 1993.
Taylor, John Russell: *The Second Wave. British Drama for the Seventies.* London: Methuen 1971.
Thomsen, Christian W.: *Das englische Theater der Gegenwart.* Düsseldorf: Bagel 1980.

Books on contemporary British drama in school

"Fremdsprachliches Theater in der Schule." (Themenheft). *Der fremdsprachliche Unterricht,* Heft 86, 1987.
Groene, Horst/Schik, Berthold (eds.): *Das moderne Drama im Englischunterricht der Sekundarstufe II.* Königstein/Ts.: Scriptor 1980.

Media

Film:

Educating Rita. Produced and directed by Lewis Gilbert. Rank Classic Collection (Video). Available at Schauinsland Medien GmbH, Postfach 20 04 30, 44634 Herne.

Pygmalion (Video). Available at the British Council, Hahnenstr. 6, 50667 Köln, Tel. 0221/20644-0 (-36 Videothek).

Acknowledgements

P. 9 Taken from: "Contemporary British Dramatists" by W. Russell, Copyright (c) 1994. St. James Press. All rights reserved. Reproduced by permission.

P. 10–11 "The Willy Russell Story", Sheila Kay Fund, Liverpool.

P. 12–13 Excerpt from: "What's the Use of Educating Women?" by Edward D. Eddy in *Saturday Review,* 18 May 1963.

P. 30–32 "Does Accent Matter?" by John Honey, London: Faber & Faber 1989, pp. 174–175.

P. 32–34 "What Was That You Said?" by Tom McArthur in *Newsweek,* 26 April 1993. (c) Verlagsdienst Newsweek, Postfach 10 24 04, D-69014 Heidelberg.

P. 53–55 Review by Simon Howard. By kind permission of *Plays & Players* magazine.

P. 55–56 Review by Rowena Goldman. In: *drama, The Quarterly Theatre Review,* October 1980, published by the British Theatre Association.

P. 56–57 Review by Clive Hirschhorn. In: *Sunday Express,* 24 August 1980. (c) Express Newspapers/Distr. Bulls.

P. 73–74 "Pygmalion Revisited with a Scouse Accent" by Geoffrey Hutton in *The Australian,* 23 April 1983. (c) *The Australian.*

P. 84 Excerpt from: "The Common Pursuit" by F.R. Leavis. By kind permission of Author's Literary Estate and Chatto & Windus.

P. 86 Excerpt from: "My Liverpool Home" by Sarah Allen. By kind permission of Dinosaur Publications Limited.

P. 87–88 Excerpt from: "This is Liverpool". By kind permission of the Merseyside County Council.

P. 89–90 Excerpt from: "Plays I" by W. Russell, London: Methuen Drama, Random House 1996. Reprinted with kind permission.

P. 106–107 Excerpt from: "Two Cheers for Democracy" by E.M. Forster, Harmondsworth: Penguin 1974, pp. 115–116.

The editor and publishers are grateful to the authors, publishers and others who have given permission for the use of copyright material identified in the text. It has not been possible to identify the sources of all the material used and in such cases the publishers welcome information from copyright owners.

987 654 321